DYNAMITE
ONLINE TEACHER

Dynamite Online Teacher

110 Tips, Tools & Ideas to Connect With Your Students Online and Embrace Progress

Dennise Heckman

Published by Game Changer Publishing

ISBN: 9798562858689

DOWNLOAD YOUR FREE GIFTS

Read This First

Just to say thanks for buying and reading my book, I would like to give you a free bonus gift, 100% FREE, no strings attached!

To Download Now, Visit:

http://www.DynamiteOnlineTeacher.com/dh-freegift

www.PublishABestsellingBook.com

DYNAMITE
ONLINE TEACHER

110 Tips, Tools & Ideas to Connect With Your Students
Online and Embrace Progress

Dennise Heckman

www.PublishABestsellingBook.com

Dedication

To my family, thank you for all your support, encouragement, and belief in me.

Foreword

How do students learn best? This is a question we have been asking for as long as education occurs in our world. Intervention, enrichments, strategies, safety nets, and other tools have pointed us to two indicators for success: high, consistent expectations and engaging experiences. Without one, you can't have the other.

COVID-19 brought new words to educators' word banks. Synchronous, Asynchronous, Blended, and Online Learning will be the buzz words for 2020. With these new words comes a need to find practical and intentional strategies to support high expectations and student engagement.

Dennise has crafted a resource for educators to engage students virtually with tools and strategies that can be utilized tomorrow in classrooms, live and online. **Dynamite Online Teacher** starts with an overview of where we have been in education and a challenge to move forward in innovative and researched based ways. Dennise's insight, advice, and ideas are relevant for this time and moving forward towards deep and lasting learning online. So while we will continue to find resources to elevate student learning, **Dynamite Online Teacher** will be a book you will be able to reference now and in the years to come.

Jessica Cabeen

Principle of Ellis Middle School, Austin, Minnesota. Author and national speaker, Jessica was awarded the NAESP/ VINCI Digital Leader of Early Learning Award in 2016 and in 2017 was named the Minnesota National Distinguished Principal. You can visit her at: https://jessicacabeen.com/about/

.

TABLE OF CONTENTS

INTRODUCTION

Who is this book for?

This book is written for all the dedicated teachers busy adapting lessons, previously planned for in-person teaching, to online lessons. The teachers, rolling with the punches and staying afloat, in unfamiliar territory with limited guidance and often lack of support. Teachers that are passionate about their subject matter but aren't sure how to demonstrate that from a computer screen. Teachers that want to reach out and connect with their students with whom they previously shared laughs, interests, and daily mood swings. Teachers who hung little winter coats on hooks under displays of student work and teachers who opened their classrooms to students needing a place to go before or after school. Some of you know these teachers, work with them, live with them, raised them, or are one of them. This book is for the teachers who are sad about moving to virtual education because they are "in-person people" and can't imagine how this new career in teaching will look. I'm right there with you. Lots of teachers are in this place of uncertainty, frustration, and concern.

Simply put, this book is for educators. While the book focuses on teachers and online teaching, it also acknowledges that educators come in all shapes and forms. Whether you work with toddlers or teenagers, whether you're writing curriculum, or standing in front of a classroom, whether you've been an educator for 20 years, considering entering the profession, or just interested in education, this book might have something for you.

While a large portion of this book focuses on practical solutions, such as virtual platforms that can improve your online classes, it also touches upon the emotional aspects of teaching. You will learn how to incorporate humor into your teaching and accommodate all of your students regardless of their learning styles. You'll also learn how to take care of yourself: how to address perfectionism-based anxiety and cope with the fear of failure. You'll get tips for self-care routines and how to improve your work-life balance.

A healthy work-life balance is something many people struggle with. On the surface, it would seem teachers have *less* of a problem. After all, how can you compare having summers off, to working day-in and day-out all year round, right? The statistics show a different story, though. A 2018 teacher wellbeing survey found that 74% of education staff, reported that the inability to switch off from work is one major contributing factor to a negative work-life balance. Bringing work home blurs the separation between work and "real life" - especially when you're teaching online and working from home. All that vacation time doesn't seem to count as time off - another study found that teachers end up working on average 53 hours a week.

Teachers often find that a healthy work-life balance is hard to find. A bulk of a teacher's work is done outside of class time. Planning lessons, grading essays and tests, thinking up new ideas, and getting familiar with new tools and technology. When these things aren't considered part of official working hours, they blend in with other parts of life - sometimes even taking the place of essential things like socializing time and self-care.

Many teachers end up burnt out and often leave the profession. One in five teachers intends to leave the profession, saying that they feel overworked. Burnout and an unhealthy work-life balance end up hurting not only the individual, but the economy and in turn, society as a whole. According to the Harvard Business Review, about 190 billion dollars per year is spent to address the psychological and physical effects of burnout. Burnout is the direct result of not having a healthy work-life balance.

The switch to online work might make finding a healthy work-life balance even more challenging. The average person checks their text messages every six minutes. Working from home is made more difficult when your home isn't built for it, or when you have roommates or partners who also need to work from home. Working from home is especially distracting if you're going to be looking at the pile of laundry that still needs to be done and doubly so if you have kids at home who suddenly don't have a school or day-care to go to. Add to that, figuring out a whole new teaching method. The only question that remains is: how can you *not* be overwhelmed in such a scenario?

This book intends to help ease some of that overwhelm. We tackle this with information, understanding, and practical tools and tips. Hopefully, you'll feel more confident using technology to improve your lessons. You'll feel more equipped to connect with your students virtually. You'll also gain some tips for leaving perfectionism behind and taking better care of yourself outside of work.

The switch to online teaching can be extremely daunting and overwhelming when you're a new teacher or used to in-person teaching. Let's tackle this challenge together.

What is the purpose of this book?

The demands of new technology, emerging seemingly overnight, are changing the way we view education and teaching as a career. I have met certified teachers of Generation Z (born roughly between 1997-2012) that have no intention of ever teaching in a brick and mortar building. They have already set up camp somewhere on the web, on an educational platform, or created their own website and space to teach online.

Online learning and teaching is something which many teachers stuck away on a shelf somewhere. This idea gathered much dust over time, and for many, this remained just a thought. In 2020 we were suddenly jolted into the reality, where this once thought needed to become active. I want to take educators through some of the positive aspects related to learning and teaching online.

When a teacher looks at what is required to be successful in online teaching, it's important to know how the facets of this process are put together. It is imperative to remember the learning and teaching cycle has not changed. It is still a case of teaching a concept, demonstration by applicable examples, some formative activities, test for retention of understanding, and then finally summative assessment. Each of these aspects is covered in a virtual classroom.

Teaching a new concept in a traditional classroom involves a few key factors, including having the correct aids to assist you in the teaching process. Depending on the school, this could range from having the most basic needs met with a whiteboard and markers, to sophisticated classroom technology such as smart boards and Chrome books. How can this be done in the virtual classroom?

The most important thing to acknowledge, is that there is still a need for teaching aids. The main difference now, is that these aids must be digital to make them accessible in your new environment. Fortunately, many platforms are available for educators to choose from and most of the platforms are accessible at absolutely no charge. If this seems daunting, then it's also good to know, that help is always at hand in the form of user groups, YouTube videos, and even personal online instructors. As a teacher on this virtual journey, you are not alone.

The online learning environment provides a rich assortment of tools and platforms from which teachers can tap into. Many of them may suit your situation with minimal modification. You can share demonstrations with virtual students by having them log into online resources directly or as downloaded material. It's also good to know that there might be occasions, where teachers can share relevant examples without having to prepare the example themselves.

Formative assessment is an area where teachers can call on different types of activities in a physical classroom. Options include individual assignments, working in pairs, or groups. These activities can be done as self-investigative projects to emphasize important concepts. As a teacher, you might ask, but now what do I do? We're working virtually.

In an online classroom, you can still carry out formative activities. It's a matter of being open-minded and not being afraid to dive in and learn how. Many platforms will allow students to work on an assignment together in a shared environment. This is made possible by tools that permit students to text and video call in real-time. Teachers are able to set time limits when a particular activity must be completed. My daughter's college professors do this with her online quizzes. Taking it a step further, some of these formative assessment platforms will also track actual student login and working time.

It's a fact that many classroom environments have a mixed bag of students. Teachers often need to provide extra time for some learners and provide more challenging material for students who get bored quickly. As with many of the proceeding questions, teachers are not sure if this can be done in the virtual classroom.

Teachers are left with choices. They can develop their material for different learning styles. If you don't have the time, or feel you don't have the capability, you can find something for all learning styles on the internet. There are many sites that offer resources in all subject areas.

Summative assessments are probably one of the most challenging areas in the online classroom, and rightly so. These activities are often exit tickets for grade and subject levels. One of the glaring problems is authenticity. Final summative assessments often include a variety of activities, from short questions to long-form text answers. Can this be done online?

Fortunately, a lot of work has been done, and many of the barriers which were there when online learning was in its infancy, have been eradicated. Today, most platforms are designed to minimize authenticity fraud. Students are also not limited in the way that they submit their work. Online assessments are possible, and are used in many environments globally with a great deal of success.

Educators are often set in their ways and simply thrive on structure. The introduction or forced move to online teaching has thrown many educators into the deep end. I've heard that things are going to be different. Personal contact may not be possible in some circumstances. But, there are digital tools and platforms out there for every phase of the learning and teaching cycle. Educators need to have an open mind and not be scared to ask for help.

This book is a compilation of my research and experiences in online teaching and those of many teachers I've talked with, or observed. My hope for you reading this book is that you gain the information, tools, motivation and confidence to teach virtually and that you have fun along the way. At the end of each part of this book, there are discussion questions. They are great conversation starters in a group setting and also help for individual reflection. The action items are meant to get you moving and set goals to incorporate a few of the ideas provided. Do not feel obligated to implement every idea in this book. Narrow down your favorite ideas and decide which ones will most benefit your particular students. I've also included a short story at the end of each of the six parts of this book, to provide insight into what changes teachers have gone through over the years and how they embraced the change. The stories and characters are fictional and meant only to entertain and inspire.

WHY did I write this book?

A love of learning, researching, and teaching has always been with me. As a kid, I would set up a "classroom" in my parent's basement and beg my little sister to "come to school", so that I could organize activities for her and have her check books out of my "library." Every book on my bookshelf had a handwritten, sign-out paper stuck into its pages. On occasion, I laugh at finding one still stuck in an old copy of *Frog and Toad Are Best Friends,* or *Misty of Chincoteague.*

After studying fine art at the Savannah College of Art and Design, I transferred to a state college, back home in Pennsylvania, to acquire my teaching certificate. Kutztown University arranged for me to privately tutor adult English language learners. This is how my teaching career began, as an ESL (English As A Second Language) teacher at a non-profit, literacy council. To my surprise, I found that helping people learn something that they wanted and needed so badly, was far more rewarding than creating art for my own sake. That was back in 1995, and I still cherish a holiday ornament given to me by a woman from Vietnam, at the Literacy Council.

Education and my higher degree meant a ton to my family, particularly my mother. She attended college at the same time that I did, after years of working difficult jobs in production. On both my mother's side of the family and my father's side of the family, I am among the first generation to attend college. Not because my grandparents, parents, aunts and uncles weren't college material. They're hard-working, creative, entrepreneurial and inquisitive people. Higher education just wasn't an option, not until two of my cousins and I headed off to our college campuses in the late 1980s and broke the glass ceiling. To me, education is a privilege, and I remind my two teenagers of this often in hopes of instilling respect and appreciation for their own teachers and the opportunities their schooling provides.

Teaching art education in middle school and high school for seventeen years taught me that a lesson is only as engaging as its presentation to the students. I found that my students became more engaged and excited about my curriculum when I presented the material in a way that 1. Have students set personal educational goals, 2. Allow for self-directed education, 3. Connect the curriculum to the students' lives, making it relevant to them, and 4. Involve students in their own critique and assessment.

I still teach, though no longer in a brick and mortar classroom. Teaching in a virtual classroom has its own set of challenges and rewards, but still provides me with a place to help students explore and grow. I wrote this book partly to organize and research the multitude of apps, websites, instruction, and tips bombarding me every day on social media and in conversation with other educators, but also to demonstrate that this change we are in the midst of, this adjustment to virtual education can be done. And because of what I know of teachers (that they are resilient and persevering), the adaptation of online learning will be made, and it will be done fantastically.

WHEN is a good time to implement the ideas in this book?

Yesterday! Just kidding. It doesn't matter if you've been teaching virtually for years, or just getting your toes wet. You're at a great place to begin implementing the tips, tools and ideas described in this book. Like many industries and careers, there's always going to be change and learning required. And there is no better time than right now to embrace the change and add some new ways to connect with your online learners. And just a little side note here... some things never change... like your intent to help students grow and learn. I've also found that clear communication, consistent routines, giving students a choice, and incorporating both synchronous and asynchronous learning activities continue to be important and needed in a virtual classroom.

Join Us on Facebook

Join Other Readers of *Dynamite Online Teacher* at facebook.com/dynamiteonlineteacher.

On our Facebook page, readers can connect with other teachers preparing for a career in virtual education and teachers already knee-deep in virtual education. Ask questions about the tips, tools and ideas in this book, share experiences and find empathy and motivation. I check the page frequently to interact, answer questions and post new ideas and tips I gather from other teachers and sources. I look forward to connecting.

PART 1

What progress have we made in American education?

The goal of Part 1 is that you become more familiar with the changes in American education and how the changes became milestones of progress. My ultimate hope is that you remain open to the changes coming your way and enjoy some of the changes with an open heart.

The advent of the 21st century has brought many revolutions in the world, and majorly in the technological sector. The staggering progress in technological innovations has not only created changes in one or two sectors, but has transfigured the entire working mechanism of various fields. It can be seen in history that many meaningful shifts occur in society, when unpredicted happenings force the widespread experimentation around any latest notion. During World War II, when American men stepped out for the war, women handled all the men's work and proved successful. Women never stepped back after that. It is said that humans naturally resist change, but the truth is humans do not naturally oppose the change. They accept the changes when they believe it's in their best interest to do so. One of the major impacts of technology can be witnessed in our educational sectors. All of the educational sectors have introduced digitalization in tasks, due to which teachers and students are now encouraged to practice their educational activities on various online platforms. This transition is also one of the results of the 2020 pandemic. The integrity and reputation of education, as well as of teachers, depends upon the ways through which you deliver effective online lessons.

For the successful implementation of students' online learning experiences, it is vital to provide professional development, time, and technology resources. If you get all essential elements together in an effective way, you can provide relevant instruction and strong learning opportunities. For this, teachers have to become capable of building the following:

Understandable guidance and expectations. This is important for students when the teacher is not present in the room to track their work.

Various resources that support learning, such as "micro-lectures." This puts the long material into small and logical modules; online videos, multimedia presentations, readings, interactive online explorations and offline hands-on activities. Through varied tools, students can learn and grasp the concept properly, and empower the teacher to enhance the students' learning experience.

Teachers are responsible for guiding each student towards achieving learning goals. For this, they need to monitor the progress of every student and identify when and where they need more support. This can be accomplished through personalized instruction, providing students easy and compatible pathways through the content, by offering different ways for students to finish tasks and providing tools and resources for students with learning differences or learning disabilities. For students to be effective online learners, communicators, and collaborators, it is important to model and facilitate online exchanges that deliver the best ways for them to interact and work online.

- Check Lynda.com for short videos about how to work in a learning management system (LMS).
- Use OERs (Open Educational Resources). OERs are full of videos, articles, case studies, examples, and many other information tools that prove helpful for you and your students.
- YouTube is a great source for teachers.

- Creative Commons is also good to check out.
- Game-based learning sustains the attention spans of students and forms a sense of community when used a classroom tool.

With this all being said, try to embrace the change, but don't be hard on yourself. Try new experiments, make mistakes, learn from it, and have fun. Teaching-with-technology in this era is like engineering the plane while flying it. But remember, you are not alone in this journey. Your students, their parents, your family, colleagues, and friends are all pulling for you. For students, the most important thing is not your technical expertise but your teaching passion.

From the seventeenth century and into our twenty-first century, sprinkled across decades, these turning points brought challenges and unwanted upheaval to communities, teachers, and students. But change is not always a necessary evil. It all depends on how you view the change.

Change arrives in many shapes and sizes and at different times in our lives. Sometimes a small change has a big impact but you can't put your finger on it; you just know, there's no going back. In no way is this story representing a huge or tragic change in my young life, but I remember it clearly and it may have prepared me for the many changes coming my way in later years. At the age of ten or eleven, my father and I were driving along a back road that passed the beautiful Pennsylvania farm fields. Stretched out across the rolling hillsides, the fields slopped into a wetland and eventually came to a stream lined with wild raspberries. On many hot August afternoons, I had picked these wild raspberries with my mother. Now, gigantic, earthmoving vehicles tore up the fields and construction crews scrambled around the area. Our truck came to a stop. I squinted my eyes to see a man holding a road sign. I asked my father what was happening and he said, "They're building homes." I sat up taller on the bench seat and asked, "But what about the raspberries?" The tanned road worker turned his stop sign and waved us on. My father drove on slowly and said, "Things change." And that was that. Many of my school classmates grew up, got married and now live in that field of homes, raising their families and doing good in their community.

"Without deviation from the norm, progress is not possible."

Frank Zappa

CHAPTER 1

What does progress in American education look like?

Let's take a look. A timeline of progress in American education is presented here. The timeline was compiled, written and is updated by **Dr. Edmund Sass, Professor Emeritus of Education at the College of Saint Benedict/ Saint John's University**. Dr. Sass has granted me permission to include his timeline to demonstrate progress in education. Please note that this timeline is not exhaustive of educational progress in general nor of Dr. Sass's timeline, and is instead a careful selection of events that I felt contributed to the growth and change leading us to the embracement of online learning. Dr. Sass's timeline is much more extensive and includes many more important and critical events than the timeline presented.

PROGRESS IN AMERICAN EDUCATION

What does progress in American Education look like? Let's take a look.

1620

The Mayflower arrives at Cape Cod, bringing the "Pilgrims" who established the Plymouth Colony. Many of the Pilgrims are Puritans who had fled religious persecution in England. Their religious views come to dominate education in the New England colonies.

1635

The first Latin Grammar School (Boston Latin School) is established. Latin Grammar Schools are designed for sons of certain social classes who are destined for leadership positions in church, state, or the courts.

1636

Harvard College, the first higher education institution in what is now the United States, is established in Newtown (now Cambridge), Massachusetts.

1638

The first printing press in the American Colonies is set up at Harvard College.

1638

Hartford Public High School opens in Hartford Connecticut. It is "the second oldest secondary school in the United States."

1640

Henry Dunster becomes President of Harvard College. He teaches all the courses himself!

1647

The Massachusetts Law of 1647, also known as the Old Deluder Satan Act, is passed. It decrees that every town of at least 50 families hire a schoolmaster who would teach the town's children to read and write and that all towns of at least 100 families should have a Latin grammar school master who will prepare students to attend Harvard College.

1690

John Locke publishes his Essay Concerning Human Understanding, which conveys his belief that the human mind is a tabula rasa, or blank slate, at birth and knowledge is derived through experience, rather than innate ideas as was believed by many at that time. Locke's views concerning the mind and learning greatly influence American education.

1690

The first New England Primer is printed in Boston. It becomes the most widely-used schoolbook in New England.

A BRIEF HISTORY OF
PROGRESS IN AMERICAN EDUCATION

What does progress in American Education look like? Let's take a look.

1783

Because of his dissatisfaction with English textbooks of the day, Noah Webster writes A Grammatical Institute of the English Language, consisting of three volumes: a spelling book, a grammar book, and a reader. They become very widely used throughout the United States. In fact, the spelling volume, later renamed the American Spelling Book and often called the Blue-Backed Speller, has never been out of print!

1785

The Land Ordinance of 1785 specifies that the western territories are to be divided into townships made up of 640-acre sections, one of which was to be set aside "for the maintenance of public schools."

1787

The Young Ladies Academy opens in Philadelphia and becomes the first academy for girls in the original 13 colonies/states.

1789

On December 11, The University of North Carolina at Chapel Hill was chartered by the North Carolina General Assembly. It is the only public university to award degrees in the 18th century.

1801

James Pillans invented the modern blackboard.

1827

The state of Massachusetts passes a law requiring towns of more than 500 families to have a public high school open to all students.

1836

The first of William Holmes McGuffey's readers is published. Their secular tone sets them apart from the Puritan texts of the day. The McGuffey Readers, as they came to be known, are among the most influential textbooks of the 19th Century.

1837

Louisville, Kentucky appoints the first school superintendent.

PROGRESS IN AMERICAN EDUCATION

What does progress in American Education look like? Let's take a look.

1839

The first state funded school specifically for teacher education (then known as "normal" schools) opens in Lexington, Massachusetts.

1852

Massachusetts enacts the first mandatory attendance law. By 1885, 16 states had compulsory-attendance laws, but most of those laws are sporadically enforced at best. All states have them by 1918.

1856

The first kindergarten in the U.S. is started in Watertown, Wisconsin, founded by Margarethe Schurz. Four years later, Elizabeth Palmer Peabody opened the first "formal" kindergarten in Boston, MA.

1857

The National Teachers Association (now the National Education Association) is founded by forty-three educators in Philadelphia.

1867

The Department of Education is created in order to help states establish effective school systems.

1867

Christopher Sholes invents the "modern" typewriter. Known as the Sholes Glidden, it was first manufactured by E. Remington & Sons in 1873.

1873

The Society to Encourage Studies at Home is founded in Boston by Anna Eliot Ticknor, daughter of Harvard professor George Ticknor. It's purpose is to allow women the opportunity for study and enlightenment and becomes the first correspondence school in the U.S.

1876

The Dewey Decimal System, developed by Melvil Dewey in 1873, is published and patented. The DDC is still the world's most widely-used library classification system.

1897-1902

1897-The National Congress of Mothers is founded by Alice McLellan Birney and Phoebe Apperson Hearst. It becomes the National Parent Teacher Association (PTA).

1902-A youth program begun in Ohio "is considered the birth of 4-H." With the passage of the Smith-Lever Act in 1914, 4-H becomes a national program for positive youth development. .

1909

The Columbus Ohio School Board authorizes the creation of junior high schools. Indianola Junior High School opens that fall and becomes the first junior high school in the U.S.

A BRIEF HISTORY OF

PROGRESS IN AMERICAN EDUCATION

What does progress in American Education look like? Let's take a look.

1916

Louis M. Terman and his team of Stanford University graduate students complete an American version of the Binet-Simon Scale. The Stanford Revision of the Binet-Simon Scale becomes a widely-used individual intelligence test, and along with it, the concept of the intelligence quotient (or IQ) is born. The Fifth Edition of the Stanford-Binet Scales is among the most popular individual intelligence tests today.

1917

The Smith-Hughes Act passed, providing federal funding for agricultural and vocational education. It was repealed in 1997.

1919

All states have laws providing funds for transporting children to school.

1926

The Scholastic Aptitude Test (SAT) is first administered. It is based on the Army Alpha test.

1938

Laszlo Biro and his brother Georg patent the ballpoint pen.

1939

Frank W. Cyr, a professor at Columbia University's Teachers College, organizes a national conference on student transportation. It results in the adoption of standards for the nation's school buses, including the shade of yellow.

1944

The G.I. Bill of Rights officially known as the Servicemen's Readjustment Act of 1944, was signed by FDR on June 22. Some 7.8 million World War II veterans take advantage of the GI Bill during the seven years benefits are offered. More than two-million attend colleges or universities, nearly doubling the college population. About 238,000 become teachers. Because the law provides the same opportunity to every veteran, regardless of background, the long-standing tradition that a college education was only for the wealthy is broken.

1946

Recognizing "the need for a permanent legislative basis for a school lunch program," the 79th Congress approves the National School Lunch Act.

1959

The ACT Test is first administered.

A BRIEF HISTORY OF
PROGRESS IN AMERICAN EDUCATION

What does progress in American Education look like? Let's take a look.

1963

Samuel A. Kirk uses the term "learning disability" at a Chicago conference on children with perceptual disorders. The term sticks, and in 1964, the Association for Children with Learning Disabilities, now the Learning Disabilities Association of America, was formed. Today, nearly one-half of all students in the U.S. who receive special education have been identified as having learning disabilities.

1965

Project Head Start, a preschool education program for children from low-income families, begins as an eight-week summer program. Part of the "War on Poverty," the program continues to this day as the longest-running anti-poverty program in the U.S.

1971

In the case of Pennsylvania Association for Retarded Children (PARC) v. Pennsylvania, the federal court rules that students with mental retardation are entitled to a free public education.

1971

Michael Hart, founder of Project Gutenberg, invents the e-Book.

1972

Texas Instruments introduces the first in its line of electronic hand-held calculators, the TI-2500 Datamath. TI becomes an industry leader known around the world.

1977

Apple Computer, now Apple Inc., introduces the Apple II, one of the first successful personal computers. It and its offspring, the Apple LLE, become popular in schools as students begin to learn with computer games such as Oregon Trail and Odell Lake.

1981

IBM introduces its version of the personal computer (PC) with its Model 5150. It's operating system is MS-DOS.

1983

Columbia College begins admitting women. Though Columbia University had been awarding graduate and professional degrees to women for many years, this change of allowing women to enroll in Columbia College as undergraduates makes it the last Ivy League school to become completely coeducational.

1985-1989

Microsoft Windows 1.0, the first independent version of Windows, is released, setting the stage for subsequent versions that make MS-DOS obsolete.

1989 - The University of Phoenix establishes their "online campus," the first to offer online bachelor's and master's degrees. It becomes the "largest private university in North America."

1989

Mumford High School in Detroit, Michigan becomes one of the first schools in the United States to install Metal detectors to improve school safety.

A BRIEF HISTORY OF
PROGRESS IN AMERICAN EDUCATION

What does progress in American Education look like? Let's take a look.

1990

Teach for America is formed, reestablishing the idea of a National Teachers Corps.

1991

The smart board (interactive white board) is introduced by SMART Technologies.

1992

City Academy High School, the nation's first charter school, opens in St. Paul, Minnesota.

1994

CompuHigh Whitmore is founded. It claims to be the first online high school.

1994

Jim Clark and Marc Andreessan found Mosaic Communications. The corporation is later renamed Netscape Communications. On December 15th, they released the first commercial web browser, Mozilla 1.0. It is available without cost to individuals and non-profit organizations. By the summer of 1995, more than 80% of internet users were browsing with Netscape!

1994

Whiteboards find their way into U.S. classrooms in increasing numbers and begin to replace the blackboard.

1995

Georgia becomes the first state to offer universal preschool to all four year olds whose parents choose to enroll them. More than half of the state's four year olds are now enrolled.

1998

Google co-founders Larry Page and Sergey Brin set up a workplace for their newly incorporated search engine in a Menlo Park, California garage.

2001

The controversial No Child Left Behind Act (NCLB) was approved by Congress and signed into law by President George W. Bush on January 8, 2002. The law, which reauthorizes the ESEA of 1965 and replaces the Bilingual Education Act of 1968, mandates high-stakes student testing, holds schools accountable for student achievement levels, and provides penalties for schools that do not make adequate yearly progress toward meeting the goals of NCLB. .

2003

The International Association for K-12 Online Learning (iNACOL), a non-profit organization dedicated to enhancing K-12 online education, is "launched as a formal corporate entity."

CHAPTER 2

How did major leaps of progress in American education impact teachers?

Just like progress in all aspects of our daily living affect how we think and feel about our world, our community, and ourselves, major leaps of progress affect teachers. Change is often the end of something and the beginning of something else. Sometimes change happens suddenly without warning and sometimes it presents itself so slowly that without realizing we've made a gradual shift. Sudden change is the most difficult for obvious reasons, but sometimes the writing was on the wall and we ignored it and that change was on its way before we acknowledged its presence. We fear change when things are comfortable and recognizable. Even when people are unhappy with their circumstances they fear change. This demonstrates that people would rather feel certain about things than feel happy about things. As **Scott Mautz, author of Find the Fire**, says, "Uncertainty registers in our brain like an error does. It needs to be corrected before we can feel comfortable again, so we'd rather not have that hanging out there if we can avoid it." Mautz goes on to address what he refers to as the 4C's of change; career, competence, case and core. He says, "Fear of change is one of the single most career-limiting moves you can make. You must believe you have the competence for change. If you're not clear on why the change is being instituted, get clear. And lastly, find your anchor and recall what the pending change WON'T change about your world that's important to you."

Growing up in a Disney family meant lots of trips around the **Carousel of Progress** in Tomorrowland at Disney's Magic Kingdom. The carousel had a huge impact on me the first time I watched it's six theaters circle around in 1976. Walt Disney had created the show to demonstrate the progress of electricity to be featured in the General Electric Pavilion at the 1964 World's Fair in New York. The idea of change is presented as progress demonstrated through the lives of a middle-class American household from approximately 1900- 1985. Change can be tough. Some people crave it and most cringe at the thought of it swooping into their lives and wreaking havoc on all the order they've managed to put in place. But, take a look back at the changes in American education throughout history from 1600 through the present day, and view the changes as pure progress. The stories of American educators throughout the time that I have included at the end of each part of this book are written in tribute to the Carousel of Progress. For inspiring me to look back at history with the excitement and fascination a person of that time period would have looked forward with.

CHAPTER 3

What can we learn by looking at progress in American education?

1. Tip: History repeats itself.

Looking back at history, it may be easy to say, " I figured that (insert a change) would be successful and I knew that (insert change) would never work." But at the time, there's really no way of knowing how it will all end up. It's no secret that we repeat our mistakes, sometimes over and over. It's human nature. The same battles have been fought, the same wars waged over religion, politics, love, family, revenge, land, money and the list goes on. Why do we care? Because American Education will repeat successes and mistakes as well. You either embrace the progress or try to stop it, which will only slow it down, maybe.

2. Tip: Deep and lasting learning comes from the sharing of ideas & knowledge.

- Use daily or weekly informal assessments and encourage student feedback and discussions regarding the lesson.
- Use questions to begin the lesson.
- Your role as a teacher needs to shift to the facilitator. If in-person, move around the classroom. My class was most productively engaged and resulted in the most creative

masterpieces when the room was a noisy, messy, seemingly out of control space.

- Seek opportunities to collaborate with other students, classrooms, and experts. Incorporate interviews, surveys and secret ballots.
- Design lessons with multiple learning paths to engage all learners and their different learning styles. Be sure to incorporate text, images, video and audio components to each lesson.

3. Tip: When students produce something, with their knowledge, it increases ownership of learning in-person and online.

When a student researches a topic, and finds a fact, they will take ownership of that fact, and remember it for a much longer time than if the teacher had just given them that fact. If the student is asked to share the fact that they found, the chances of them remembering the information skyrockets. Giving students the time to find the fact on their own can be time consuming and it would certainly be much faster to write the fact on the whiteboard and say, "Here it is, the fact of the day, copy it down and memorize it." But this gives the student no ownership, no responsibility and no connection to the fact. History has repeatedly demonstrated that when someone learns something or better yet, experiences something on their own, they are deeply connected to the new information. For example, listening to a teacher's lecture on details and facts of the Civil War cannot have the impact that makes students write a story from the perspective of a Union soldier on the first day at the Battle of Gettysburg could. Now the student gets a chance to choose which information is interesting to them and include it in their story. Each student will interpret the research in their own unique way and present that interpretation in their story. Their stories will provide teachers insight that lecturing could not possibly bring about.

4. Tip: Students remember very little of what has no relevance to their daily lives. Connect your virtual lessons to your online students frequently.

Now let's say the students have written their Civil War soldier stories and perhaps shared them. How can we make the experience of the Civil War soldier relevant to the lives of our students? The goal here is to decide what is the fundamental idea of the lesson? Is it to remember rote facts, names and dates? Probably not. Most history teachers hope that their students feel as moved and passionate as they do when teaching a topic such as the Civil War. Well then, go for the emotional and the personal. Ask the students, " What kind of a person is your soldier?" Have students interview a family member, friend, teacher or community member about their experience as a soldier. As a group, have students list qualities of a soldier. Look at the list and have students write the name of someone they know next to each quality on the list. For example: strong- Dad, Smart- my sister. This activity brings the story of their soldier home. There are so many ways to tie the guiding principles and important elements of your lesson to the lives of your students.

CHAPTER 4

How can we apply what we learn from history to our virtual classrooms?

5. Idea: Ask students how they can learn from people's past endeavors and progress.

Have students research a specific time period or event and find someone that interests them. Ask them to imagine getting a one on one interview with that historical person and write the interview questions they would want to ask. Now, have them find the best answers to their own questions by researching that historical person.

6. Idea: Have students share their new found knowledge in a blog or tweet.

Students are posting their images, messages and lives all over social media. It is natural for them. My two teens can't imagine life without this instant sharing of thoughts, expressions, ideas and opinions. Connect their learning to this, by having them post/ share their research, interviews and newfound information, in a class blog or class Twitter account. There are also several apps and websites listed in Part 4 of this book that work well for this sort of sharing and posting of information, images or video.

7. Idea: Assess students on what they can do, with what they know.

How about this idea... ask students what they can DO with the new knowledge they have. Have them take action and demonstrate what they can do with this newly learned information. After all, applying knowledge is the goal, isn't it? Not just sitting on, saving it for another day, or hoarding it all for ourselves. Knowledge is better spread around and shared. So have your students do SOMETHING with what they know.

8. Idea: Connect examples of human progress, recklessness, humanitarian efforts, prejudice, advancement, etc. to relevant and current popular news and media.

Ultimately, students want to learn. Drive all their new knowledge home by having your students find, list and discuss relevant examples in their world today with examples from history. Narrow the time of history they can look back to or open up the whole can of worms!

Let's meet Theodore - Teacher at the Boston Latin School, Boston, MA.

"It looks like the robins are getting ready to celebrate spring today. What year is it? Oh, 1693. And believe me, things couldn't be any better in American education than they are today. Just take this classroom, there are fourteen wooden benches for my students and I have all the light I could need beaming in through the window. Yes, sir, I'm happy to teach in such a fine school. It's been seventy-three years since my Puritan grandparents arrived in Cape Cod and set out with other families to establish educational counsel here in the New England Colonies. By 1635, their third eldest, my father, was enrolled right here, where I teach, in the first Latin Grammar school established in the Colonies, The Boston Latin School. From what he told me, other boys his age with fathers working in the church or courts attended. After grammar school, my father was sent to the public High School that opened in Hartford in 1638. Well, he and his friends had big plans to attend Harvard College, over in Newtowne. Harvard was the very first higher education institution and at that time, the only one. In 1640 Henry Dunster became the President of

Harvard AND taught everything. Unbelievable! But just this year, the College of William and Mary was established down in Virginia Colony. Boy, oh boy, two universities! The Massachusetts Law of 1647 mandated that every town with over 50 families hire a schoolmaster to teach their children reading and writing, and that every town with over 100 families hire a Latin Grammar schoolmaster to prepare their students for Harvard College. It's no wonder both my father and I are Harvard alumni. And, isn't the printing press a dream machine, I mean in 1638 they set that marvel up at Harvard College and now we have reading material like John Locke's *Some Thoughts Concerning Education*, to refer to, and that's his second published book. And thanks to progress three years ago, they published The New England Primer for my students, which makes my life as a teacher much simpler."

Discussion Questions

- Do you view changes in education as progress? Always? Sometimes? Rarely?
- How has progress in the twenty-first century affected your curriculum?
- Has progress in the twenty-first century been a positive experience for you as a teacher?

Action Items

- Take extra time to discuss and support the relevance of your topic to your students' lives.
- Ask a teacher that has been teaching for much longer than you, "What changes occurred during your career as a teacher?" You may find that while you were a school student, your teachers' changes were difficult and you were unaware.
- Look at one particularly hard change in your teaching career and find someone in another career sector to discuss its effect on them.

Fun Fact

Do you know what Sylvester Stallone, Gene Simons, Mr. T and Sting all have in common? They were all teachers before their entertainment careers took off!

References

Sass, Edmund. (Updated March, 2020). *American Educational History: A Hypertext Timeline.* Retrieved August 2020 at:

http://www.eds-resources.com/educationhistorytimeline.html.

Mautz, Scott. (Nov. 16, 2017). Science Says This Is Why You Fear Change (and What to DO About It). Retrieved August 2020 at:

https://www.inc.com/scott-mautz/science-says-this-is-why-you-fear-change-and-what-to-do-about-it.html

PART 2

How Do I Engage Students Online?

The goal of Part 2 is to demonstrate that your students want to be engaged, are open to being engaged in online education, and it is possible to engage students in every online lesson you teach.

A student is more open to engaging in an activity if they take part in the activity's creation. If students are given the opportunity to explore their own curiosity, they will initiate their own learning. Being curious about a topic has magical effects, like falling in love, wanting more time, seeking more answers. Want to add another magical element to your classroom and lessons? Get excited! Yes, you. As the teacher, you need to display boatloads of enthusiasm for your own subject. It may seem obvious, and MOST teachers are intoxicated by their topics and their exuberance rolls off their tongues and into the hearts of their students. BUT every so often one of my own children says, "It seems like Mr. "So and So" just doesn't like being a teacher. He seems bored or something."

Let's face it, not everyone is a natural entertainer, and can perform a musical-like lesson plan in front of their class complete with a colorful personality, wit and humor every school day of the year. But, if you are actually interested and still intrigued by your topic, it shows and the students absorb your enjoyment in presenting the material.

"It is our choices, Harry, that show what we truly are, far more than our abilities."

J.K. Rowling

The Dynamite Teacher's

Quick Tips for
Engaging Students
Online

1. HELP YOUR STUDENTS SET MEANINGFUL EDUCATIONAL GOALS
2. NARROW YOUR TOPIC
3. COVER THE FUNDAMENTALS
4. TURN ALL TOPICS INTO QUESTIONS
5. TEACH FOR IMPACT BY TELLING STORIES
6. GET STUDENTS INVOLVED IN THEIR OWN ASSESSMENT AND EVALUATION.

Add some magic to your curriculum...
Be enthusiastic when you present your material!

CHAPTER 5

What are the Best Online Practices to Get Results?

9. Tip: Help Your Students Set Meaningful Educational Goals

Why set goals? Goal setting is similar to creating a daily to-do list. As you cross off each item, you feel like you accomplished something for the day.

Goals give you something to look forward to and to work for. Because goal setting gives you a purpose, they help with anxiety and boost your confidence. A goal has a plan of action and a result.

Goal setting is key to a child's personal growth and professional success, as setting goals will be an inseparable part of their lives. Each aspect of their lives will require goal-setting skills, from which school or profession they will choose, how they will handle relationships, or adjust to life transitions.

A goal is not always something you want, however. It's a list of things to do. It's an action plan for the day. When you wake up in the morning and make your daily to-do list, is it a list of things you want? No, it's a list of things to do. It's an action plan for the day. For some reason, when asked to list goals, goal setters often only want desires to show up on the list.

A list of goals may include a few desires sprinkled in, such as, "Go on vacation," but that goal needs a sub-list titled, "What I need to do to go on vacation." This sub-list would be more effective at springing you into action because it would break down the going on vacation into small tasks like, "Hire a dog sitter, buy airline tickets, ask off work, and more."

To boost their productivity, effectiveness, and satisfaction, teach your students to set SMART goals.

SMART goals are:

- Specific (sensible, significant)
- Measurable (motivating and meaningful)
- Actionable (achievable)
- Relevant (reasonable and realistic)
- Time-bound (time-sensitive)

When you teach your students to set SMART goals, you help them bring their goals closer to reality.

Ask your students to create a list of goals for each project or each unit of your course and explain how to write an actionable goal. For example, instead of your student writing, "Pass the test," have them list, "form a study group, complete the study guide, create flashcards." Now they get to cross off tasks as they complete them, and each time, they will feel one step closer to passing that test.

The SMART checklist helps your students evaluate their goals and plan the actions that will help achieve them.

To add accountability to goal setting, have students share their goals by posting, blogging, or privately sharing with classmates or family members.

10. **Tip: Narrow Your Topic**

Narrowing your lesson topic is always important, but becomes vital in virtual education. Narrow topics are more suitable for online communication and are more comfortable for your students to research and discuss from a computer screen.

When teaching online, you may have less instruction time, less one-on-one time to communicate with students, and your students have less contact with each other to discuss a broader topic.

Stick to what is relevant, as too much information can create confusion the same way too little information does. Appropriate and straightforward instruction leads to greater understanding, effectiveness, and productivity.

Teach your students how to use time management to plan their activities and organize time for learning. This should help them learn to identify productivity patterns, set priorities, and increase confidence.

Use a graphic organizer to narrow your topics into bite-sized lessons. The inverted triangle or pyramid always works well as it allows you to present the most critical information first and keep the broader topic at the top of mind for the future. The inverted triangle model helps engage and grab the students' attention and draw them into the subject.

Also, narrowing your topic will likely result in sticking to the fundamentals, which leads us to...

11. Tip: Cover the Fundamentals

You know the story. You walk into class and announce the new topic with enthusiasm. Sure enough, a hand goes up in the back of the class. You sigh, knowing exactly what the question will be but ask anyway, to which the student replies, "Why do I need to know this?"

This will certainly still happen while teaching online. Schooling has become about the mastery of a vast body of information. And much, if not most, of this information, will in most cases, never be needed in the student's life.

The problem here is not about teaching what the student may not need, but because we are missing the lessons they will likely need—for example, finances, relationships, work ethic, and more.

This is where that mental list comes into play. We have so much to do, so much to say, so much to teach. Our goal is to teach our students awe-inspiring information and hear them have "Ah-Ah" moments, but we run out of time, and many of the fundamentals get pushed to the wayside of our curriculum. We end up just trying to get through the day, the week, the semester, and the year.

A student of mine had expressed that she wanted to measure her grandmother's baking pan but didn't know-how. For many years after, I taught sixteen and seventeen-year-olds taking two and three AP courses in other subjects, how to use a twelve-inch ruler. Whatever your subject is, narrow your topics and be sure to teach the fundamentals. Your students will remember you for this.

Be precise about what you want your students to learn, check with them for understanding and provide multiple examples.

Online engagement allows you to present the information in a fun and captivating way that sparks student curiosity. It enables you to access a wide range of interactive and practical lesson plans that cover your topic's fundamentals and engage your students in online education.

12. Tip: Turn All Topics into Questions

Phrase your lesson topics in questions. Think of the who, what, when, and where of your topic. Add questions such as, "Would you rather this or that?"

Questions are precious tools in teaching as they encourage critical thinking and more answers demonstrating the depth of understanding. Most teachers are familiar with the goal of Bloom's Taxonomy to move students from memorization to higher-level thinking. The cognitive skills that help students learn are (in the hierarchical order, based on their complexity):

- Remembering
- Understanding
- Applying

- Analyzing
- Evaluating and
- Creating.

The most demanding cognitive process is creating with new knowledge. When we teach our students new information, we want them to take it with them and relate it to other areas of their lives.

Encourage the growth mindset in your students. Children with a growth mindset are curious and see mistakes as learning opportunities. They are ready to take healthy risks and are continually stimulating their brains with new challenges. Also, students with a growth mindset can handle constructive criticism because they are focused on continuously improving themselves.

On the other hand, kids with a fixed mindset tend to believe that their skills and intelligence are fixed and cannot be improved. They avoid changes and efforts and tend to give up easily when confronted with life challenges.

The growth mindset will help your students set SMART goals and put effort into achieving them. These qualities will also help your students explore and learn with confidence because they are not afraid of failures but identify the obstacles and find constructive ways to overcome them.

13. Tip: Teach for Impact by Telling Stories

Students have told me the dandiest things over the years. Kids love sharing stories about their everyday lives and experiences. Stories aren't just for bedtime. And they aren't just for children.

Storytelling has become a necessity in marketing and sales. Businesses rely on storytellers to sell their services and products. The narrative of someone's small business is what will gain loyal clients. When we were kids, we shared stories about our school days; as adults, we now share information about our students, clients, patients, and more.

It is believed that the oldest form of storytelling is represented in Chauvet cave in France, dating 36,000 years ago. Later, around 700 BC, the first written story by the Greeks appeared. But there were many stories told within families and passed from one generation to the next verbally. For example, it is believed that Aesop's Fables were passed along verbally for three hundred years before being written down.

How did storytelling become so important? Think of the Civil War, for example. If stories had not been verbally passed on and written down in cherished letters home and sacred journals in the war camps, what would we know? If the few existing photographers in the 1860s had not shown up on the battlefields, the Civil War story would have been Gone with The Wind. And we would not have Scarlett O'Hara to share her story.

Today, storytellers are highly regarded and often highly paid people. They are our screenwriters, commercial writers, playwrights, authors, news reporters, bloggers, radio personalities, and songwriters.

Students connect emotionally to stories. Stories spur students' curiosity about the world around them, boost creative thinking, and spark interest in the topic.

When you tell your students a story of your own experiences, it enables them to privately imagine how they would respond in the same situation without repercussions. Stories give us time to anticipate, contemplate, and process information. No matter where you travel in the world, you will find storytelling. Storytelling is universal.

14. **Tip: Get Students Involved in Their Own Assessment and Evaluation**

What is student self-assessment? Well, it can be as simple as having your online learners give you a thumbs-up to show their grasp of the lesson and that they are ready to move on to the next step or stage of the activity.

Or, self-assessment can involve an intensive journal writing activity. Depending on the subject, grade level, learning style, and goal of the lesson, self-assessment takes on many different aspects.

Self-assessment in pre-school children may involve asking them to circle a face with a smile or a face with a frown to indicate how they feel about the activity.

On the other hand, college-level self-assessment must dig for a deeper understanding and evaluation by enhancing performance. Self-assessment should promote and allow for self-correction and improvement; otherwise, it may not be beneficial.

Coming from a career teaching high school art, formative assessment is natural and expected. My art students would complete a project and then self-evaluate in four categories; craftsmanship, effort, technical ability, and originality.

Their self-evaluations were then turned in with their projects and taken into consideration when I completed my assessment. The students were honest and often wrote extra thoughts or pertinent information next to their scores. This process gave me insight and connected me to their learning experience in a way that I could not have had otherwise.

Self-assessment is a vital ingredient of formative assessment. In the virtual classroom, formative assessment increases student motivation, achievement, and independence.

The purpose of student self-assessment is to provide feedback that improves performance and offers an opportunity for adjustment and correction.

To enhance your students' self-assess, provide examples of mastery so your students get to know what excellent work looks like. Provide your students with the specific vocabulary that will help them evaluate their work. Encourage the students to share their voices, give constructive feedback, and treat each other with respect.

In today's classroom, I can imagine the creative ways teachers could have students present their self-assessments rather than on a piece of paper.

Use savvy apps and technological tools such as self-assessment question cards, emoji worksheets, exit slips, lesson tweet slips, etc. that could stimulate your students and make the self-assessment process even more intuitive and fun.

CHAPTER 6

How Can I Teach For All 4 Learning Styles?

The following tips and ideas apply to both in-person and online education. All learning styles can be accommodated virtually with a bit of knowledge and creativity.

15. **Tip: Visual**

Visual learners learn by looking at information, seeing it in front of them, or their minds. They tend to come across as impatient and may talk fast, covering many topics with many descriptive words and phrases.

Visual learners love maps, charts, timelines, diagrams, graphic organizers, presentations accompanied by power points, and lots of images or videos. They can "eye things up" when hanging a picture on the wall or choosing a paint color or a particular outfit. They are spatially intelligent and understand how things fit together without measuring.

An excellent Visual Learning Activity to teach your students involves Vision Boards.

Visualization or mental rehearsal is a technique in which we imagine ourselves in a particular situation or performing a specific activity. You can teach your students to use visualization to view themselves reaching their goals.

The visualization shows the best effects when applied through vision boards. A successfully created vision board focuses on things your students want to achieve, but more importantly, it emphasizes how they feel.

Vision boards provide clarity and incentive and inspire action.

Other examples of suitable Visual Learning Activities may involve:

- Art
- Creating a PowerPoint presentation
- Illustrating a book they read
- Decorating cookies

Older visual learners may also enjoy designing and painting a community mural, helping the theater teacher create and paint the stage scenery, and helping you rearrange your classroom or decorate your bulletin board, so make sure to encourage these activities.

16. **Tip: Auditory**

Auditory learners learn by listening. They tend to speak slowly and are patient listeners. Their thought process is linear, and they prefer to have someone explain or teach information to them verbally rather than have to read it or look at it in visual form.

Auditory learners love talk-to-text functions on their cell phones and computers, and they enjoy technology like Alexa and Siri.

Text-to-speech App converts text into spoken words. When the user enters the text, the application reads it aloud (speaks).

Although initially developed to support visually impaired persons and people with reading impairments such as dyslexia, today's text-to-speech applications have extensive use in online interactive teaching and learning.

To successfully teach aural learners, be sure to incorporate verbal explanation with PowerPoint presentations or any other visual tool.

Examples of Auditory Learning Activities:

- Listening to podcasts
- Story time
- Special guest speakers
- Verbal directions
- Verbal project requirements
- Verbal instructions, music, lectures, and speeches

Also, older auditory learners enjoy having in-depth discussions and listening to foreign languages and accents.

Bimodal Presentations

Young learners benefit the most from bimodal or mixed presentations. Students will retain more information if presented both visually and in audio format simultaneously (bimodal presentation).

Bimodal presentations often include text-to-speech software.

For example, research has proven specific benefits of bimodal presentation in learning to read.

Some of the main advantages of bimodal presentations include:

- Enhanced learning and memory
- Improved information recall
- Greater reading comprehension
- Improved word recognition and vocabulary, accuracy, and fluency
- Increased self-confidence
- Improved concentration.

17. Tip: Verbal Learners

Our verbal learners prefer the written text over pictures and listening to someone tell them information. They are the readers and the writers, and the note-takers during your PowerPoint presentation or video.

These students enjoy any writing prompt and most writing techniques, whether an essay, short answer, or full book report. They read quickly, and words flow for them smoothly when relaying a story, directions, or any information. If this student is working with peers, they will be the ones turning another student's verbal idea into a written explanation.

An excellent verbal learning activity to practice with your students is journaling or expressive writing.

Journaling involves writing our thoughts, observations, and feelings without censoring them. This helps us understand our thoughts and feelings more clearly, validate our experiences, and increase our inner world's awareness.

Journaling can spark your students' imagination, remove mental barriers, inspire them to think out of the box and find creative solutions to problems.

Moreover, writing down their thoughts without auto-censure can help your students cope with specific mental health concerns and improve their overall well-being.

Other examples of Verbal Learning Activities to practice with your students include:

- Learning to read
- Reading different materials such as newsletters, magazines, brochures, instructions
- Writing stories
- Writing educational or factual material
- Watching foreign films with subtitles
- Making lists, labeling
- Writing in a secret diary
- Putting a message in a bottle

Older verbal learners enjoy activities such as presenting story time to smaller children, story mapping, and fiction writing.

18. **Tip: Kinesthetic**

Kinesthetic learners learn by doing. They are the action-takers. These students take their time making decisions and talk slowly and thoughtfully. They prefer to engage all of their senses to learn something new and love to solve problems. Their approach always involves some hands-on activity, and they are open to trial and error.

Encourage free play, particularly in younger learners, because play engages all senses, sparks imagination and creativity, and promotes development. Play encourages brain development, promoting the growth of new neural connections, and enhancing the brain's plasticity and flexibility.

Play and exploration boost language development and improve motor skills.

Moreover, unstructured play promotes problem-solving skills, helps students explore cause and effect relations, anticipate and predict outcomes, learn cooperation and communication skills, and work through conflicts.

Also, hands-on activities allow students to cope with unpleasant emotions and learn positive ways to communicate their feelings and needs.

Sensory and craft activities encourage students to follow their interests and to express themselves freely.

Sensory activities help create and strengthen connections in the brain's neural pathways. This supports students' cognitive and language development, problem-solving, and gross motor skills.

Tactile and craft activities promote fine motor skills and hand-eye coordination. Also, these activities encourage creative thinking and foster social and emotional development.

Examples of Kinesthetic Learning Activities involve:

- Building Blocks
- Cooking
- Crafts
- Science Lab
- Tactile Activities
- Physical Activities
- Sidewalk Chalk Learning

Older Kinesthetic learners enjoy being tutors, sports coaches, outdoor guides, and teachers.

Other Learning Styles

Some learning experts claim there are an additional four learning styles.

Logical – Logical learners are math wizards and learn better while applying logic and reasoning.

Social – Social learners learn by explaining and teaching information to a group. This builds their own understanding of the material they are presenting. They enjoy being a part of a group for most of their learning.

Solitary – Solitary learners learn best when they have a chance to be alone and study at their own pace with only their own companionship.

Combination – You might have guessed by now that the combination learner had to be on this list because you have already identified more than one learning style you relate to. The combination learner category, which most people fall into, simply means that you learn best utilizing two or more learning style strategies.

Let's meet Benjamin- Teacher at The Young Ladies Academy, Philadelphia, PA.

"Whew, doggies, is it ever hot. It shouldn't surprise me, it is July. What year is it? Oh, 1838. And believe me, things couldn't be any better in American education than they are today. A lot changed after education became a function of the states, rather than our federal government in 1791 when the Bill of Rights was passed. A decade ago, Massachusetts passed a law requiring towns of more than 500 families to provide public High School to all students. Now, more children than ever have the opportunity to learn, and the resources we have keep getting better. Just take these wonderful student books, the McGuffey Readers. Even though they were only published three years ago, I was able to obtain several dozen copies. We also have copies of the *American Spelling Book* written by Noah Webster in 1783. I'm currently teaching a unit on the Land Ordinance of 1785, which stated that the newly expanding western territories be divided into townships expected to set aside land for public schools. Yes, change is in the air. This very school where I teach is a remarkable example of change itself. It opened in 1787 as the first academy for girls. The Young Ladies Academy is where my mother and her younger sister studied. Talking of change, out in Ohio, a college in Oberlin is now coeducational; perhaps some of my students will go onto higher education. It wasn't too long ago that the only public university to award degrees was the University of North Carolina at Chapel Hill. And thanks to progress, in 1801, a fellow named James Pillans invented what we call a blackboard. I have one here in front of my classroom. All of this talk of change makes me wonder what else will be invented to make my teaching better."

Discussion Questions

- Do you encourage and discuss educational goals with your students? Always? Sometimes? Rarely?
- How have you implemented activities for all learning styles into your curriculum?
- Is having students assess themselves something you are comfortable with as a teacher?

Action Items

- Have your students complete a self-assessment for a project or assignment. Afterward, ask students, "Were you honest on your assessment? Was it difficult to be honest? Did you enjoy assessing yourself? Would you change the way you completed the project/ assignment if you could re-do it because of what you learned from the self-assessment?"
- After incorporating activities for all learning styles into a lesson, ask your students which learning style activity they enjoyed the most, felt they did the best at, and which gave the most difficulty.
- When a lesson is completed have your students write a reflection on the learning goals they had expressed prior to the lesson.

Fun Fact

Do you know how long teachers have been hearing the excuse, "The dog ate my homework," from students? Since 1905!

PART 3

How Do I Connect with My Students Virtually?

The goal of Part 3 is to demonstrate that your online students are open to connecting with you virtually and that there are ways to connect that will create similar experiences and bonds to those in a brick and mortar classroom.

So, why are you reading this book? For one reason or another, you are teaching online, and you need to know how to connect with your students. If you've taught online, you know the challenges. Students vanish from the screen, fall asleep, prop up toys in front of the screen, have their pet attend class, crashing noises are heard off-screen, family members wander behind your students, you see and hear things that you wish you hadn't and the list goes on and on. And you wonder if you are having any real impact and if your students are learning and retaining the information you desperately try to relay over the shaky Wi-Fi. Yes, and yes. You are having an impact and your students are learning. But what about the connections you yearn for. If you have no built in face to face meetings with your students there are other ways to establish individual connections. As **Sergiy Movchan, co-founder of Raccoon Gang,** says, "There are a number of proven ways to work around the problem:"

- "Introduce Yourself: Establish a sense of interaction and connection between the students and yourself by arranging an introductory discussion. Request your students to develop a personal and quick mood board."

- "Humanize Your Course: A humanized course is more likely to develop a relationship with the students and this can be achieved in the following ways: *Leverage online discussions and Enrich Multimedia with Personalization.*"
- "Create Cooperative Learning: In this instructional strategy, a small group of students works together on a common project or task."
- "Create a Choice Option: Nothing could be more engaging than allowing a person to become a part of the decision making process. To make this happen, you may use SurveyMonkey to learn about students' opinions."
- "Enable Interactive Communication: Real-time communication platforms develop a sense of connectedness and control amongst the students. So whenever possible, try both asynchronous and synchronous forms of communication with your students."
- "Find Your Student Reward: Rewards may be timed challenges or simply to reach an achievement level. Another way to engage the students is to take their opinion in deciding the prize."

Connecting with students online is about acknowledging the differences between in-person and virtual education. This is a new territory and thus calls for new action. Moving to online education for even half of the teaching you do, is a challenge. Teachers are struggling with a lot of change coming all at once. Professional development training for teachers on remote instruction has been spotty, and some teachers feel confined by the microphone and computer setting. This is understandable. Familiar resources have become obsolete or simply removed. Constant change is unnerving and can feel like a dust storm that won't quit. Do you want to forge on and be the best teacher you can be regardless of the circumstances? Of course you do, that's why you are reading this book, hoping to find the motivation, support and ideas to move you forward.

Students are also facing tremendous change and new pressures with the move to online education. When asked what their biggest concerns were with learning from home on a computer, most students said sharing the family computer. Many talked about lack of internet access or poor internet connections. Some mentioned the noise and distractions at home and lack of privacy or a quiet place to listen. The last concern may come as a surprise to some. A percentage of older students in middle and high school said that their younger siblings often depended on their guidance and support with online education from home. Because of this, the older students admitted to sacrificing their own time and energy to help their siblings instead of doing their own school work. This situation is more common in households where there is an age gap between siblings, and adults cannot be present during online learning. You can connect with students by acknowledging the sometimes difficult circumstances that evolve around online learning. Let them know about your Wi-Fi glitching sometimes and how your cat likes to jump onto your desk and land in front of your laptop camera. Be careful not to complain or compare circumstances. Just be honest, and your students will appreciate your awareness.

How about beginning class with a rap song?

Not only will you surprise and entertain your students, but you can teach them almost anything with the lyrics of a rap song, even math concepts. Part 3 covers ways to connect with your students online. Yes, you are connected by Wi-Fi, but this is about connecting on a personal level.

How about sending your students snail mail? Receiving a physical piece of mail can be priceless for a student stuck at home with little or no contact with friends, teachers or anyone other than who they reside with. They can hold the mail, display it on the refrigerator and look at it for weeks as a reminder that you are a real person that cares. Take a selfie with your pet and have it printed on a postcard from an online site that can do this for a fair price. Handwrite a message on the back and send it off to your class.

How about setting your Zoom background to a different place each day and seeing if your students can guess where you are? Encourage them to set new backgrounds each day as well and show off some of their favorite places. If you are using a different platform than Zoom, print off pictures of your favorite places and hang them behind you.

We have all stood in front of the mirror to rehearse what we are going to say in an important conversation or for a presentation. Well, most people have, and if you've never done this, it does help. Teachers have expressed to me that part of their anxiety about online teaching is the basic idea of being on camera and being recorded. Being uncomfortable in front of the computer can prevent you from connecting with your students. If you were thrust into the online teaching world without any preview of how you would look and sound on camera, it's not too late to pause and practice. Science has proven that practicing in front of a mirror or in this situation in front of your computer camera is a helpful method of self-analysis, activates your senses and eases anxiety about being seen or heard as awkward or whatever else you may think about yourself. And guess what? As an added bonus, science also proves that having your students talk to themselves in front of the mirror or computer screen increases their reasoning, logic and problem solving with the concepts being spoken. Calling on students during online education to repeat information being taught, answer questions, ask questions or discuss topics, increases their memory of the information and provides a deeper connection between the speaker and the listeners just like in-person instruction.

During a graduate course titled *The Kinesthetic Classroom*, I learned how important "brain breaks" are in both brick and mortar classrooms and virtual settings. Students spend a long time in their seats. To give students a break from academic overload, a brain break should be purposefully incorporated into each lesson. The goal of the "brain break" is to encourage a recess from routine, incorporate fun and humor, provide bodily movement, and simply give the brain a break. From an outsider's view, these brain break activities may appear as just games, but each planned break engages the senses, reduces stress and increases circulation. The best part? "Brain breaks" escalate the connections made between participants! Why? Because engaging the senses, moving your body and having fun, even if through a computer screen, boosts endorphins, which scientists believe have a bonding effect in our social lives. And don't worry about the physical space between you and your students. It has been proven that watching and listening to a comedian on a television screen increases endorphins enough to increase a person's tolerance to pain. And, if the person watching the comedian is aware of other viewer's enjoyment, their own tolerance to pain increases even more. If the viewer can hear the laughter of other viewers, again, their tolerance to pain increases. And this is all accomplished through a television screen. So, ask your students to get out of their seats and stand behind their laptops for a few minutes. Lead them, or better yet, ask a student to lead the class in a brief kinesthetic activity. Just standing up and yawning prevents our oxygen from getting stale. You will all feel better physically and more connected socially after a "brain break."

How else can teachers connect? Reach out to your community of co-workers and parents to express your intention to work together. Build daily routines and practices and prioritize compassion over the curriculum. Teaching online is exhilarating and rewarding if you can figure out how to balance one on one face time and group face time with independent work time where students complete work and turn it in by a certain deadline.

"Alone, we can do so little; together, we can do so much."

Helen Keller

CHAPTER 7

How Can I Be The Virtual Teacher My Students Need Me To Be?

You know down deep inside that you are a teacher motivated by the need to give and help students learn whatever it is that you teach. Maybe teaching was always there in the back of your mind, or perhaps the idea went off like a light bulb one day. Maybe you consider teaching your calling. The definition of a calling is " a strong urge toward a particular way of life or career." But *why* do you want to be a teacher? The answer may help you better understand *how* to be the best teacher you can be. As **Matthew Lynch, author of The Edvocate.org,** says, "The most common reasons people decide to become a teacher are:"

1."A desire to work with young people. Some people simply like working with children because of their lively, curious, and idealistic nature, while others want to play a role in building America's future."

2."An interest in subject matter and teaching. Having a passion for what you are teaching will encourage your students to be passionate about it as well, which will assist you greatly in teaching the information. You may also be passionate about the process of teaching and learning in its own right."

3."Influence from former teachers and family. Some of you decide to become teachers after one or more positive experiences with a former teacher. Others become teachers because of family influences, particularly when a family member is a teacher, or the family holds the teaching profession in high regard."

Although Mr. Lynch is speaking of becoming a teacher in general and his statements are not specifically about teaching virtually, the core reasons for teaching carry over. How can knowing why you chose teaching as a career help you connect to your online students? Because understanding where your passion stems from gives you focus and direction. For example, if you have a desire to work with lively, curious young people, play this up and incorporate the ideas listed below in numbers twenty-three (Use a puppet to help teach your lesson!) and twenty six (Dress up like a famous or historical figure you are teaching about!). If your subject matter is your motivation for teaching, utilize the idea below in number twenty-two (Get really excited about your students' work! Brag about it, share it, and display it.) If you teach because of the influence of a former teacher or family member, incorporate the idea listed below in number thirty (invite a special guest teacher, retired or active, to speak to your virtual students, they may turn your students into aspiring teachers!)

The list of ideas included in this book is in no way exhaustive of the creative concepts possible in an online setting. You've selected this book because in some capacity, at some point you either are teaching online or considering teaching online. And you want to be the best virtual teacher you can be. Your students need you to step up and gain the skills and gather the gumption and all of the creativity you can to be the teacher they need to succeed at your subject. Both teachers and students need to adapt to remote learning platforms to ensure career and college readiness. Processes, programs, and policies for remote learning need to be understood. Every teacher needs to have access to the necessary tools to implement their lessons and also assess for learning. Seek support and training when you are feeling overwhelmed. Your students will benefit from your effort.

The following are some tips to be sure you are on the right path.

19. Tip: Consider your students' perspective! Inquire about their fears, opinions, and goals.

My daughter is in college and has had dramatically different learning experiences with her professors online. Many of the professors build time into their scheduled Zoom meetings to address each student on the call by name (builds connection), and ask them how they are and what they've been up to outside of class. At both the beginning and end of my online classes, I address each student with, "First name, do you have any questions or anything to share?" Sometimes a kid just wants to get something off their chest and often asks a question that others may also need to hear. Another great way to establish connections in the virtual classroom is to begin your lectures with an icebreaker or ask the students a random question to get to know them better. Being a good teacher is about more than teaching good lectures; it's also about establishing a personal relationship with your students. Ask what their opinion is every chance you get, it reinforces their value. And whenever possible, have students write privately. This could be in the chat box. Let them speak about their goals for the class, the lesson, or the course. As **Elizabeth Stein, teacher, instructional coach and blogger on MiddleWeb**, says, "We want to set students up so they develop that determined resiliency they need to be successful. Setting goals, then evolving and redefining goals as the realities of learning unfold through our actions." Goals can absolutely be incorporated into a virtual classroom setting and either shared or kept private. Goals shouldn't be a once and done activity; they should be evolving and not as stagnant or judgmental as resolutions. Resolutions often lead to disappointment and feel burdensome. Goals are meant to motivate and encourage actions. Be sure your students understand the difference.

20. Tip: Ask students to work together remotely to solve a problem.

There are many ways to have students working remotely, work together. As **Marci Lentnek Klein M.D., pediatrician and product designer of 3Dux/Design,** says, "By offering multiple opportunities for remote student collaboration, students not only receive the emotional benefits of peer engagement, they also prepare themselves for the more global workforce of the future where they can be effective communicators and collaborators in any setting." Klein goes on to say, "To increase the focus on student collaboration, educators can employ 3 strategies to help their students learn how to socialize and navigate relationships and in a remote setting."

1."Model positive social skills and relationship building in the virtual classroom."

2."Engage students with relevant, real-world problems that they must solve with a group of peers."

3."Allow your virtual, live classroom to be driven by student dialogue versus "teacher talk."

If your online teaching platform is Zoom, it is also worth mentioning that Zoom has a feature called "Breakout Rooms." You create a few separate virtual rooms for your groups to go to and meet away from your main meeting room. If you aren't working on Zoom, there are plenty of other methods and several apps and tools listed in this book to aid in collaboration among virtual students.

21. **Tip: Demonstrate expectations.**

Demonstrate everything you would like your students to do. As an art teacher, demonstrations are part of every new lesson I teach but demonstrating benefits all learners of all subjects. Math teachers regularly demonstrate how to solve problems and physical education teachers frequently demonstrate new skills in the weight room or on the sports field. Allowing students a chance to see you in action performing the task that you would like them to try, fulfills the needs of the visual, aural during the presentation, and the needs of the kinesthetic learner once the skills are put into practice by the student. Also, I have had students ask questions that I may not have thought to address while demonstrating. Do you fear demonstrating in front of your class? Occasionally messing up while demonstrating, has connected me to many students after sharing a laugh. Students need to see you make mistakes and shrug it off with confidence. Knowing that you can mess up, means that you are not perfect and that forms a connection between you and your students.

22. Tip: Use your student's work as exemplary examples.

Outstanding student work is a gift. It represents your hard work as a teacher and the expertise and creativity by which you presented your material. Displaying student work in any capacity is a compliment to your student for trying hard and exceeding expectations. Just because you can't staple their work on a physical bulletin board, doesn't mean you can't display it. There are countless ways to present student work online. During class time work can be shared voluntarily by students that want to hold their work up to their computer camera or read their work aloud. If students want to share their work with you privately they can meet you in a Zoom breakout room, email images of their work or meet after others have signed off of the platform you are teaching on. Part 4 of this book, lists several tools and apps that integrate with Google Classroom.

Bonus Tips:

Tip: Provide structure and normalcy.

Students typically experience a level of upheaval when transitioning to online classes. Create a regular routine for your students to follow; make homework due dates fall on the same days of the week, schedule daily check ins with your students, or provide your students with a calendar for each week's class schedule and assignments. If possible, use platforms that students used for in-person learning as well. The familiarity of these platforms will create a level of normalcy, despite the change to online learning. Like in-person learning, having a routine structure reduces anxiety, creates stability and establishes a deeper connection between you and the students.

Tip: Accept the Imperfections.

Settling into online teaching takes a lot of effort. There will be issues with Wi-Fi connections, problems with lectures, and some days might not go as smoothly as hoped. Accept the imperfections; learn to laugh off the mistakes and try again the next day. Make it known to your students that you are doing the best that you can. By laughing at your own mistakes, the students will feel less stress on their shoulders to be perfect at the online transition. You and your students will feel better by knowing that, despite your best efforts, there are still going to be hiccups in the learning process.

Tip: Establish a set of clear learning goals.

To reduce ambiguity in the online learning process, set clear goals that you hope your students will achieve throughout the semester. Provide them with a clear list of resources to maintain those goals, and check up with them frequently throughout the term of school to see how they are progressing. **Earl Nightingale, 20th Century radio speaker and author, once said,** "People with goals succeed because they know where they are going." Let your students know that by setting goals, they will have a successful school year. Though the methods by which they are learning have changed, goal setting will help set up your classroom for a successful year.

Tip: Create a normal stream of communication for your classroom.

One of the challenges of online learning is losing regular face-to-face communication with your students. Create a consistent method of communication between you and your students. Maybe you teach high schoolers that are active on Twitter; create a Twitter account in which you post regular class updates and assignments. Maybe email is your best method of communication; tell your students that you respond quickly to communication via email. Or maybe setting up a classroom website would be most beneficial for your course content. Regardless of the platform, find a way to maintain consistent communication so assignments do not fall through the cracks and so students avoid feeling isolated throughout the online learning process.

Tip: Find a regular time to reflect.

Mastering the online teaching world does not happen overnight and might require tweaking. Regularly reflect on your class progress throughout the semester. How are your students doing? Are they learning class content at the necessary pace? Are there things you can improve as a teacher to make the class more beneficial to the students? Are there new techniques you have not tested yet that could be beneficial? Check up on your progress as often as is necessary to be the best online teacher for your students.

"Say "Hello" with a class mascot. Address each student by their name with a greeting and goodbye. Hold an old fashioned Show & Tell Virtually. Play Dress-Up to the theme that you are teaching. Bring a "Secret Mystery Box" to your online classroom. Play Games. Have a scavenger hunt. Share class time with a guest."

CHAPTER 8

What Are Fun Ways to Connect With Elementary Students Online?

23. Idea: Say "Hello" with a class mascot.

Your mascot could be your cat or dog or a puppet. Puppets can sing, tell stories, wear silly clothes and hold objects pertinent to your lesson. Plus, you don't have to be a ventriloquist to do this because you can have your face off screen to give the puppet the stage!

24. Idea: Set aside time at the beginning of class and the end of class to address each student by their name with a greeting and goodbye. Encourage waving and virtual high fives.

If possible add a moment or two when students can say hello to each other also. This time period is vital to their connections with each other, the online community and with you.

25. Idea: Hold an old fashioned Show & Tell Virtually.

Kids will bring things, pets, food into view of the computer camera anyway, take the time to ask them about that stuffed animal, bag of chips, pencil eraser, etc. that keeps taking up their entire screen while you're teaching. For some students, this will satisfy their need to share something and they will be happier to listen afterwards. Don't forget to mute the rest of the class while each student shares, and then unmute to allow for a few questions from the class.

26. Idea: Play Dress-Up to the theme that you are teaching.

For example when my art class studied Wassily Kandinski, we all wore our snow boots and showed them to each other on screen. It was extra fun because it was 80 degrees outside. Create a schedule ahead of time to give students and parents time to gather the needed clothes and accessories. This way students show up online prepared and excited to take part in the group activity.

27. Idea: Bring a "Secret Mystery Box" to your online classroom and tease the students for the first part of class with hints.

What you place in the box should somehow relate to what you are going to teach. Give a certain number of hints and have students guess what they think it may be. After the big reveal of the object, explain its relationship to the topic and how its used or what its purpose is. Ask students to describe the object in the chat box and encourage visual, tactile and even smell and taste descriptions. Afterward, begin your lesson incorporating the object if possible.

28. Idea: Play Games that would normally be done in a brick and mortar classroom.

Attach a bingo sheet to your classroom documents for students to access ahead of time and play bingo with new words or terms they learned. For example, my students wrote out the names of nine famous artists on their Bingo card in any order, and then I pulled the names from a jar that the students could see on screen to play the game. There are ways to adapt most games played in person into virtual games.

29. Idea: Have a scavenger hunt at the beginning or end of a lesson for the students to find a particular object, or color of object, or a certain number of objects, etc. that relate to the topic covered.

Set an onscreen timer, or a wind-up kitchen timer, play music or play game show music to give them an audible cue when their time is up.

They will enjoy rushing off to find something and come back to share their treasure. This is also a great kinesthetic activity to break up a longer than usual listening activity.

30. Idea: One of my favorite ways to connect with virtual students is to share class time with a guest who can join us online.

Inviting other teachers or experts on the lesson topic is a great way to surprise students with another person's abilities and talents and present information in a way you may not have thought of doing. It also gives you a chance to play the role of co-host and interact with your students from a different angle. The guest could also bring a whole new subject to your classroom and tie it into your existing curriculum. For example, if you are teaching World Cultures, invite the art teacher or a local artist to guide your students through an art project that explores the culture you are studying. Prepare your guest ahead of time by providing a set amount of time to present and ask permission to record the meeting so that you can share it to your class website or another means of making it accessible to students and parents after the fact. Discuss the objectives of their presentation and encourage them to speak conversationally with your students and enjoy themselves.

Bonus Ideas:

Idea: Maintain classroom traditions.

One of the most challenging parts of switching to online learning is losing some of the in-person traditions that both students and teachers are familiar with. To reduce some of this loss, think of classroom traditions you can transfer over to your digital classroom. For example, if your students usually take a break every hour or so to get their wiggles out and recharge, continue doing this in your virtual classroom. Split up your lectures with an occasional break to let students stand up, stretch and regroup for a few minutes.

Idea: Schedule weekly appointments to meet with your students one-on-one.

This is especially helpful if you have never met your students in person. By finding time each week to check on your students, they will feel like you are genuinely concerned about their wellbeing and involved in their success in the class. Checking up will help to create a virtual bond between you and your students. This is also a great opportunity to check in with your student's parents and see how things are going with the transition to virtual learning.

Idea: Incorporate as much group work as possible.

Shifting to online learning can be a hard social transition for a lot of students. Because Zoom and other online platforms allow you to put students in breakout rooms, find ways to incorporate group work into your lectures. This will provide students with an opportunity to connect with their friends and to make new connections in the classroom.

Idea: Host virtual lunches with your students.

If you do not have a lot of flexibility during class hours to spend time checking up on your students, hold virtual lunches with your students. Schedule to have lunch with only a few of your students at a time so that you can virtually bond and spend time talking one-on-one with each of them.

Idea: Find reasons to incorporate celebrations into the classroom.

Record yourself singing happy birthday to each of your students on their birthdays; email the videos to their parents. Come up with themed spirit weeks and have your students participate by dressing up. Celebrate upcoming holidays with themed activities as well. Incorporating celebrations will excite your students and help them feel virtually connected to the class.

Let's meet Frederic- Teacher at the Indianola Junior High School, Columbus, Ohio.

"Boy, oh boy, I'm ready for some turkey. I have to admit Thanksgiving has become my favorite holiday. What year is it? Oh, 1910. And believe me, things couldn't be any better in American education than they are today. For example, teachers like myself get the chance to attend a "Normal School" to be taught how to teach. Seems silly, doesn't it? Anyway, I can't complain, my first year at teaching has challenged me and that preparation at the Normal School has helped. We have a lot of students here in Columbus. That's why we have the first Junior High School in the US, right here where I teach. Partly because of the attendance law. Back in 1852, Massachusetts enacted the very first mandatory attendance law and just about every state has since, including Ohio. We also have what the Germans named, "kindergarten", translates to something like "child garden", started in Wisconsin in 1856, and has spread across the states. The other new thing seems to be forming all sorts of groups. There's the National Education Association formed in Philadelphia in 1857, the Department of Education formed in 1867, and the Parent Teachers Association, a national group put together in 1897 by a group of mothers. Oh, I almost forgot about the 4H, a youth program started right here in Ohio eight years ago. One more, I just thought of, The Society to Encourage Studies at Home, it's what they call a "correspondence school" founded in 1873, from what I gather, mostly women enrolled. But here's a really neat idea this fella had to organize libraries, The Dewey Decimal System, what will they come up with next? And thanks to progress, in 1867 a guy named Christopher Sholes invented this fancy contraption, the typewriter. I have one here on my desk. I'm practicing every chance I get to type faster and faster. My students get a real kick out of the clicking. Yes, sir-e, progress has come to Columbus."

Discussion Questions

- Do you ask your students what their opinion is on covered topics? Always? Sometimes? Rarely?
- Do you build time into your class schedule for student interaction that is NOT regarded by learners as educational?

- Do you display student work in your brick and mortar classroom? In your virtual classroom?

Action Items

- Schedule one on one meetings with your students once per month, marking period or semester. Ten minutes should suffice just to check in and connect. Prepare students for the meeting by asking them to have something to share or ask. Record the meetings for liability reasons.
- Set up an online portfolio to demonstrate your expectations and display student work.
- Set up a website or utilize an app that encourages class chat and sharing. This gives the teacher an opportunity to join in and remark, ask questions and start deeper conversations.

Fun Fact

Who sang, "An apple for the teacher will always do the trick when you don't know your lesson in arithmetic?" Bing Crosby in 1939.

References

Movchan, Sergiy. (April 14, 2018) "How do you make individualized connections to your students via online learning?" Retrieved on RaccoonGang.com, August 2020 at:

https://raccoongang.com/blog/how-do-you-make-individualized-connections-your-st/

Lynch, Matthew. (November 3, 2015) "3 Reasons Teaching Just Might Be Your Calling." Retrieved on The Edvocate, August 2020 at:

https://www.theedadvocate.org/3-reasons-teaching-just-might-be-your-calling/

Stein, Elizabeth. (January 18, 2015) "5 Aids to Help Students Set Learning Goals." Retrieved on MiddleWeb, August 2020 at:

https://www.middleweb.com/20021/5-aids-help-students-set-learning-goals/

Klein, Marci Lentnek. (August 25, 2020). 3 Ways Educators can Support Peer-to-Peer Socialization in a Virtual Classroom. Retrieved on Medium, August 2020 at:

https://medium.com/the-innovation/3-ways-educators-can-support-peer-to-peer-socialization-in-a-virtual-classroom-40d64998f41f

PART 4

What Tools Should I be Using For The Best Online Experience?

Part 4 aims to present tools that will open new ways to enhance your online teaching, be creative with how you present your curriculum and feel that you are giving your students the best virtual education you can.

We all find ourselves in a situation now, where online learning and teaching are a concern for education globally. As professionals, we can look at this in two ways. It can either be a huge barrier or it can be looked upon as an opportunity. Educators should ask, how can we adapt to this new situation? How can we change each challenge into a victory?

A virtual classroom is a common space where many teachers and students engage on a daily basis. Personal contact between students and teachers is a huge concern. Some students need that personal contact with their teacher. Fortunately, there are many ways of crossing that bridge. The best approach is the utilization of video in the online classroom environment. You have the option of either choosing live video or to go for recorded video content.

Live video is a great way of overcoming the issue of personal teacher/student interaction. You can engage with your students in real-time, irrespective of where they are located. The only provision is that students have a mobile device to connect and can receive decent connectivity to the internet. This style of virtual teaching allows students the opportunity to interact with their peers and teachers in real-time and will remove many of the uncertainties surrounding the loss of contact.

Recorded videos can also be used as a way of simulating the educator's presence in class. The sound of the teacher's voice in itself can produce a sense of having a personal connection. This format of video lessons is extremely useful for explaining examples and demonstrating new concepts. The fact that students perceive a connection with their teacher, often leads to more extended periods of concentration and increases the student's ability to comprehend new and sometimes difficult concepts.

Another barrier teachers come across in running an online classroom is the amount of time spent on lessons and content preparation. It does take extra time when you are starting, but there are long term benefits. Don't only think of the time spent preparing content, but also the time saver this can become in the future.

If you put in the hours and do the best that you can, the benefits will be long-standing and will have a positive outcome on your students. Teachers have an advantage if they put in the time and effort, they will have created a resource that can be implemented many times in similar lessons in the future, and students will have the benefit of interacting with content which is of a high standard.

Many educators become shell-shocked when they hear the term virtual or online classroom. Much of this is because there is a feeling that they don't have the skills and knowledge to enter this new world. The pressure to perform, can often lead to anxiety and even depression. This does not need to be the case.

The internet is immense and in this greatness, it has changed our world into a single global village. A village is known as an environment where everybody knows each other and when in trouble a helping hand is always close by. The same goes for teaching online. What is even a greater advantage, is that a teacher can connect with an expert situated on the opposite side of the world.

We often find ourselves in situations that the amount of time needed to develop new material and content may be restricted. It's not necessary to stress about all of this. Somewhere on the internet someone might have had the same content to prepare and decided to go all the way. Often their resource might meet your requirements one hundred percent, or it may be adapted with a few minor tweaks. Finding these kinds of resources are not that difficult. Often it is just a Google search away.

Many huge storehouses have tons of material to complement your content. As an educator, you might be required to make that initial investment in time and effort. Once you have made the commitment and have the resources, it's just the task of sharing the relevant links to your students in their virtual classroom.

The great thing about sources with links is that you don't need to create them every time that lesson is part of the curriculum. It is easy to store the links in a simple document. This way, you are also able to build a list of suitable resources created by subject experts from all over the world.

A question I often hear teachers ask is, what will happen when we all go back to a normal school day again? You've been able to enrich yourself and the classroom environment with content that can live on your personal computer or online forever. The advantage is that all of this content will never be lost, but it can always be used to compliment whatever you teach in a traditional classroom. Students will appreciate your flexibility in being able to provide different ways of learning in the brick and mortar classroom.

Online learning is essentially a paperless procedure. As educators, many of us often have thoughts about conserving natural resources. Often these are actual discussions in our classroom. It is a great feeling to know that by embracing the digital movement, we are also embracing the idea of protecting our world for future generations. The amounts of paper used in a traditional classroom do not occur with digital learning. There are even some schools and institutions that have decided to go entirely paperless.

Before technology-enabled synchronous learning, most online instruction was asynchronous. With synchronous education teachers and learners meet at the same time online where there will be live instruction, communication and discussion. Prior to advances in technology, this sort of environment was reserved for in-person education and online education was asynchronous. Asynchronous instruction still has value on today's virtual platforms and can be utilized for students that need or want to work at their own pace and on their own schedules. To accommodate all learning styles, both asynchronous and synchronous activities should be included in your online curriculum, this will provide flexibility and opportunity for connections.

We all have limited time and a limited budget and so when trying to make the best of our teaching time we need to have the right resources at our fingertips. The following is by no means an in-depth look at any of the tools listed below, but instead a quick, ready to implement list. The tools chosen for this list were tested and approved by teachers like you, and not exhaustive of all the tools available. When asking teachers, we found that the following tools were mentioned most often and with enthusiasm and all teachers agreed that their students face a future where being digitally literate will be necessary.

All technology has a learning curve and its own set of headaches, but if you take a bit of time to explore a few, you will gain back that time in your teaching and feel more confident that you did in the long run. The goal of this book is not to teach you how to use all of the listed tools and apps. This book is in no way a technological guide nor am I a technology teacher. But I love technology and I embrace it and what it has done for our profession. The first time I laid my eyes on a computer was in seventh grade. There was one computer in my junior high that year. Teachers and students alike would go by the classroom where it lived and marvel at the DOS (Disk Operating System) and from what I remember there were only a handful of teachers in the building that knew how to "type a command," as they called it. Back then, "technology" was anything electronic including boom boxes, Sony Walkmans and telephones attached to the wall. If a teacher walked into the classroom and stood in front of the chalkboard with a cassette tape that he or she would proceed to play, our class would be beyond excited. Electronic gadgets were futuristic to us and rarely incorporated into the curriculum. But, that's the effect of technology on students of all generations. If you creatively incorporate technology into your virtual curriculum, students respond.

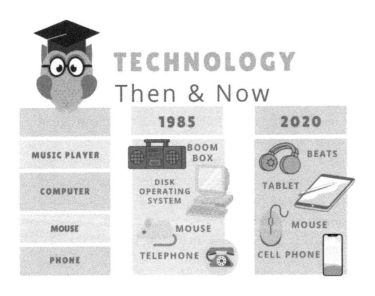

The majority of tools and apps listed below have tutorials on their sites. Most also have a boatload of YouTube video tutorials presented by the company, technology teachers and experts. Simply go to YouTube and in the search bar type the name of the tool or app and what you are trying to learn. Like magic a dozen videos in varying lengths will populate for you to choose from. Do not discredit learning from this method, if you have been fighting it. I have had many teachers ask me if this is a legitimate and trustworthy way to learn something new. The Millennials, Gen Z and Gen Alpha know that this is the fastest, most economical and easiest way to learn anything, especially technology. The fact that you can start and stop the video tutorial, replay it and try the steps they teach at your own pace, makes it straightforward.

"The tools which would teach men their own use would be beyond price."

Plato

CHAPTER 9

What are creative ways to use Zoom when teaching?

As described on the company website: https://zoom.us/

"Zoom is used for teleconferencing, telecommuting, distance education, and social relations."

Aside from all of the expected ways of using Zoom when presenting your curriculum, keep in mind that many other regular classroom activities can be done on Zoom. Here are a few:

31. **Idea: Games** - Annotation Tool Pictionary, Bingo, Chatbox Trivia

32. **Idea: The White Board** - Endless opportunities for teaching.

33. **Idea: Story Time** - Hide a story related prop in a bag and have the students guess what it is based on clues they heard read from the story.

34. **Idea: Directed Art Activities** - Based on Lesson Theme

CHAPTER 10

What should I know about Google?

As described on the company website: https://www.google.com/

"Google is a technology company that specializes in Internet-related services and products, which include online advertising technologies, a search engine, cloud computing, software, and hardware."

When we speak about Google, the first thing that comes to the mind of most people is Gmail. What many do not realize is that Google is much more than just an emailing platform. Google includes a whole suite of applications that can provide a perfect environment for online teaching.

A Google account provides you with a virtual cloud on the internet called a Google Drive. Once you register an account on Google you also have access to 15GB of storage space. This is ample storage space for most teachers running a virtual classroom. If you do run short of space, there is an option to purchase more space from the company.

The great thing about Google Drive as a teaching tool, beyond the 15GB of storage, is that it provides a convenient way of organizing your work by creating folders and sub-folders. It's possible to store practically any file type on your cloud. If you create files with one of the other Google applications, the amount of storage space you use on the drive is practically zero.

Google Drive comes with some nice file and folder sharing features. These features allow you to decide how and with whom you want to share the information. If you have information to share with your students, they will be able to view the content without having their own Google ID. Student collaboration can also be encouraged by giving students editing rights to files created in Google Apps.

Once we look beyond the storage space, teachers will also find the office suite of Google quite useful. These applications have enough power and tools to see all of the needs of most educators in the virtual learning space. There's Google Docs, which is an excellent word processor. A spreadsheet called Google sheets, and a powerful presentation program known as Google slides. As mentioned above, documents created with these programs use no physical space on your 15GB Google drive allocation. An added advantage is that you will be able to access your documents from wherever you are. All that you need is a computer or mobile device, and a connection to the internet.

Google Docs is an excellent word processing tool that can be used for all your word processing needs. It includes all the formatting tools you would expect from a word processor. You have access to the full selection of fonts. It's also possible to set up headers and footers, page numbering, tables, a table of contents, etc.

If you need to do calculations or graphing, then Google Sheets will provide you with everything you need. There are even some useful reporting tools and apps for performing different types of data analysis. It's possible to set up a database within Google Sheets as one would do in most other spreadsheets. Each file in sheets can include multiple sheets to work with.

Google Sheets is an excellent program for designing presentations for course content online. There are many built-in templates to choose from. It also includes tools for creating slideshows and will be able to take care of all of your presentation animation needs.

Google Drawing can be initialized from Google Docs. It allows you to create annotations that can be inserted into your document without having to leave the program. The drawing program is quite intuitive and easy to use.

Video lessons have become a huge component of most virtual classrooms. Google apps provide the perfect solution for your live online video lessons called Google Meet. You can initiate the application indirectly from your Gmail account. The application can interface with your Gmail contacts list seamlessly.

Teachers always need to organize and schedule classes, meetings, assessments, and so on. Google even has an application you can use to get and keep yourself organized. It is called Calendar. With this tool, it is possible to set up different calendars on the same platform. Each one can be assigned a different color code. The strength of Google Calendar is that it can interface with all of the Google applications and with many other third-party programs as well. It provides a great way of keeping yourself organized from a single program.

Teachers, whether working online or not, always need to create and utilize some sort of form. This could be to create a survey, questionnaire, or notice to parents. Google Forms offers a great way of creating any of these. It even includes enough flexibility for the creation of online assessments. An extremely useful function of Google Forms is that it can interface directly with Google Sheets. This can be used as an excellent way to collect data and information directly from forms and assessments submitted online. Data collection, collation, and analysis are simplified in this way.

Google Classroom is a great application for running an online classroom. Many schools and districts may have a Google for education license. Where this is not the case, each individual with a Google account also has free access to Google Classroom. It is a typical LMS in that teachers can set up various classrooms, share content, and assessments. Google classroom also interfaces with Google Drive as well as Google Meet.

Teachers are often unaware of what they have when they register an account on Google. They have everything in one place from where it is possible to run a fully online class, and even a complete virtual school. A free Google ID allows you access to a great emailing system, a private space in the cloud, and a huge number of built-in apps to work with. Each of these applications interfaces with each other almost seamlessly. It's also a perfect way to share information and files with students and colleagues. You don't even need to worry about backups, Google automatically backs all your work up for you on the Cloud. Also, you will be able to access your work wherever you are.

35. Tool: Google Drive

What should I know about Google Drive?

As described on the company website:
https://www.google.com/drive/

"Google Drive allows users to store files on their servers, synchronize files across devices, and share files."

- Tip: Google Drive is accessible on all devices.
- Tip: Google Drive gives you lots of FREE storage.
- Tip: Create shareable links or email files or entire folders.
- Tip: You never need to click SAVE! Google Drive Autosaves.
- Tip: Google Drive offers both folders and sub-folders.
- Tip: Google Drive allows you to color code your folders.

36. Tool: Google Classroom

What should I know about Google Classroom?

As described on the company website: https://classroom.google.com

"The primary purpose of Google Classroom is to streamline the process of sharing files between teachers and students."

Google Classroom is a fantastic Learning Management System (LMS) coming from the Google stable of applications. There are two versions;

a paid version which is part of the Google for Education Suite, and the free version which is included with every free account. Many teachers globally use this app as their platform of choice for running and hosting their virtual classroom.

The paid version forms part of the Google Suite for Education and is used by many schools and even in entire districts. This version comes with many extras not included in the free version. Institutions and educational districts can administer their server on Google. Administrators have autonomy on how many of the tools are rolled-out and which levels of the authorization will be assigned to various users, teachers, and managers.

The free version of Google Classroom is available to every person with a personal Google account. You have a total of 15GB available for running your virtual classroom, which is directly related to the available storage on your Google Drive. As an educator you are able to interface with files that are stored on Google Drive.

One of the great facilities is that every person with a personal Google account can set up a huge number of separate classes on a single Google subscription. Each tab can be color-coded or include relevant graphics. This makes it easier to find your specific classroom on the platform. It's possible to interface with each classroom separately, overall the classrooms with a single action, or with a specific group of classes.

Student registration in the free version is a simple process. Each classroom has a unique code on the Google platform. Students can be invited to choose the classroom by presenting them with the code via email or any other suitable messaging system. If you want to run a completely free learning environment, it is also possible to have a setting that every person with the code can access your class on this platform.

A Google Classroom has a few distinct Tabs which are available to teachers. The first is called the Stream and is the area where each resource, content, message, and assignment will appear. This list is organized according to the date it was uploaded by the educator. Students can view such content or information in their stream. Educators have the option to have information on the stream available for all students within a classroom or across a group of classrooms. It can be limited for an individual student or to a specific group of students.

Your Google Classroom can easily look like a disorganized teaching space if you are not careful. This is because of the way the stream is set up by default. Fortunately, your classroom has tools that allow you to organize the content you create. This can be done via date, topic, period, teaching term, or in whatever way suits you best. It's a good idea to get your system set up early on, as it is easier to maintain something than to repair.

The Classroom Tab is the area where you will create all of the resources that will be shared with students attending the class. Google Classroom allows educators to create four different types of resources. Each one has a specific focus.

The first type of resource is the Assignment tool. It is quite versatile and you can place different types of material in a single assignment. The material can be video content, PDFs, google apps files, or whatever kind of content you want to share. Assignments can even include an assessment with prescribed mark allocation.

The question resource allows teachers to create different types of questions for assessments. As with the assessment part of an assignment, it's also possible to attach a prescribed mark allocation to a question. It is possible to create different question types.

Teachers who simply want to share curriculum content with the class, it's best done using the material type of content creator.

Each of the creation tools found under the classwork tab will be seen in the student's stream. As described earlier, the teacher can decide who will have access to this content. It's even possible to set time limits and deadlines for each of the shared resources. Students are required to submit each task they are assigned to on their stream. Teachers are notified by the system as soon as a student has submitted any work.

Teachers have to react to each submitted student task or assignment. Google Classroom will allow teachers to review each assignment and also to provide students with the necessary feedback. It's extremely useful that this feedback can be given using different types of content. Teachers are also able to decide whether to provide feedback to everyone on a specific topic or assignment. You can even provide feedback to a specific student.

Google classroom also takes care of many of the time-consuming tasks associated with the collection, recording, and collation of student results. Each assignment or questionnaire is integrated into a very useful grade book. The results of each student will be recorded in the grade book automatically and Google Classroom is able to create individual reports.

Teachers can schedule when resources are made public in student streams. This is extremely useful as it allows educators to create resources and lesson plans in advance. The content can be scheduled to be visible to students according to predefined timelines.

Google Classroom also allows teachers to connect with classrooms in real-time. This is possible by using Google Meets as your video lesson platform together with Google Calendar to schedule such lessons. You can share the Calendar with classes and individual students. The system will also notify both teachers and students of upcoming live video lessons.

Google Classroom might fulfill all of your virtual classroom needs. From administration to content and assessment hosting, to reporting. With this platform in your collection, you will not need to invest in another LMS.

Google Classroom has become the go to platform for online teachers at every grade level across the globe. And it's pretty exciting to be a part of this progress. Technology can easily become the shiny object we can't get enough of and loading a lot of stuff onto your Google Classroom is fun and interactive, but not the most important part of your time spent with your students online. Try not to lose sight of connecting with your students every single time you are online with them. When teachers are asked what causes them the most anxiety about moving their teaching online, they often begin to list the things they don't yet know how to do on Google Classroom. The following list will set you in the right direction to being a dynamite Google Classroom facilitator.

- Tip: Learn how to create your Google Classroom.
- Tip: Learn how to invite students.
- Tip: Learn how to create an announcement.
- Tip: learn how to set class permissions.
- Tip: Learn how to manage multiple classes.
- Tip: Learn how to create an assignment.
- Tip: learn how to create a class resource page.
- Tip: Learn how to grade assignments.

37. **Tool: Google Slides**

What can I do with Google Slides?

As described on the company website:

https://www.google.com/slides/about/

"With Google Slides, you can create, edit, collaborate, and present wherever you are."

- Idea: Embed a Google Drive video to present it seamlessly.
- Idea: Set that video to autoplay when you reach that slide.
- Idea: Insert charts and diagrams.
- Idea: Incorporate stop motion animation.
- Idea: Publish directly to the web.

38. **Tool: Google Jamboard**

What should I know about Google Jamboard?

As described on the company website:

https://edu.google.com/products/jamboard/?modal_active=none

"Jamboard is an interactive whiteboard."

- Tip: Files are called "Jams."
- Tip: Have student groups collaborate visually on a Jam.
- Tip: You can draw and use emoji's on Jams.
- Tip: Jamboard is great for tactile learners.
- Tip: Share content and images from the web.

39. **Tool: Loom**

What should I know about Loom?

As described on the company website: https://www.loom.com/

"Loom is a video recording tool that helps you get your message across through instantly shareable videos."

Loom is a personal and convenient way to send a message without needing to text, email or write anything. It's also fast and easy and works on most devices. Businesses have been using Loom to collaborate in all sorts of ways that would otherwise be done in the office. Let's take it to school and see what we can come up with.

- Idea: Send the parents of your students a Loom "newsletter."
- Idea: Send your students a Loom evaluation of their project.
- Idea: Send your students a Loom of their homework assignment.
- Idea: Send a Loom to your substitute teacher explaining lesson plans.
- Idea: Use Loom to teach in your differentiated classroom by creating Loom messages for students working at a different pace or in a different direction.

CHAPTER 11

What Are The Must-Have Tools For Online Teaching?

Several different technologies are used in online education. It's important to acquaint ourselves with these technologies. In-depth knowledge is not essential, but it is important to have broad knowledge. This will assist us as teachers to perform our tasks as virtual educators more professionally. We will look at some of these technologies and see how these are used in virtual teaching.

The utilization of video plays a huge role in teaching online. It is seen as a key way of introducing the void left by the loss of personal teacher/student contact which is experienced in the traditional classroom. Teachers can decide whether they want to use live video or recorded video in the classroom. Each mode has a specific role to play.

Live video is a great way of simulating a live classroom situation. It is an environment that allows students and teachers to communicate in real-time. Students can engage directly with teachers and peers. A huge number of platforms are available. These include programs such as Zoom, Skype, MS Teams, etc.

Recorded video is a useful platform for teachers who are less confident in front of a camera. It does not have the real classroom-type of interaction as with live video. A great advantage is that the recorded video can be replayed when necessary. Students have the means to listen to past lessons that they did not understand. Teachers have the advantage in that they can reuse the same video for lessons in the future. Many platforms allow video recordings. These can either be stored online on various sites or can be stored on your local hard drive. Some examples of applications which allow video recordings are Loom, Screencastify, Camtasia, etc.

Screen-recording software is another useful tool for any online teacher's tool bag. These applications allow teachers to record their screen actions while working on their personal computers or laptop. Also, some of these platforms allow you to store the recordings in standard video formats which allow teachers to share their work online easily. Screen-recording software provides a great medium for explaining examples or scenarios related to concepts covered in the online classroom. The platforms discussed in the recorded software paragraph also allow screen-recording. Another useful addition to this group is a computer program called Active Presenter.

Learning Management Software (LMS) is a group of software that plays a huge part in the success of running an online learning platform successfully. Most LMS platforms can assist you in managing all aspects of teaching and learning. This includes classroom administration, lesson hosting, student assessment management, and much more. In the past several years, the number of LMS platforms available for teachers and institutions has grown immensely. Some include Moodle, Schoology, Edmodo, Clarion, and as discussed previously, Google Classroom, etc.

One of the technologies that teachers should not overlook is social media. Many of the social media platforms have tools that can be implemented successfully in virtual classroom environments. These include the likes of Facebook, Twitter, WhatsApp, Instagram, etc. Social media platforms come with a double advantage for both teachers and students. Not only do you have applications that allow you as the teacher, to communicate with students and parents, but, also an environment that many students engage with daily.

Whiteboard technology has also joined the virtual learning and teaching environment. In the past, these were physical apparatus teachers used in a brick and mortar classroom. Today there are many digital versions available. Some exist as standalone programs while others are included as part of larger online platforms. An advantage of this kind of technology is that teachers can share such a digital whiteboard with their students in real-time. It even allows two-way sharing, in other words, students can also be given the authorization to add content to the lesson. This is an excellent way of getting students involved in the lesson and can be used as a way of encouraging group discussions.

We definitely cannot forget the internet as a rich resource that can be implemented in a virtual classroom. Many of you have heard of YouTube, SlideShare, Vimeo, Khan Academy, etc. The number of platforms or sites which are available online is huge. Students can engage with material that is readily available on these sites, or with material you've created and uploaded to one of these sites.

Animation is an excellent way of creating teaching material for students that is engaging. A few years ago, animation needed to be left to the experts. Today, many applications allow teachers to create simple animations with relative ease. Some of these engines, as they are called, exist as online environments only, while some can be downloaded onto your local computer or laptop. Besides the number of standalone animation environments, teachers should be aware that virtual classroom animations may also be created on any presentation program such as Google Slides, Microsoft PowerPoint, etc.

Online Assessment Tools have also grown in stature in the virtual classroom environment. Many of these applications allow teachers to set up digital assessments which their students may do online. In many cases, the teacher can set up assessments so that they interact with online grading tools seamlessly. This takes out a lot of the pain associated with grading and collating student results manually.

Teachers who move into the online learning space are not short of technology to support them in this environment. It is important not to look at these tools in isolation, but rather to see how each one may add value to your online classroom. Take the plunge and experiment with the above listed technology and the tools and apps listed below. Soon, you'll be comfortable in both a virtual classroom and traditional brick and mortar versions.

The following list includes descriptions taken directly from the sites and apps named.

40. **Tool- Padlet-** https://padlet.com/ From the site, "Padlet lets users create endless sticky notes and post them to various wall templates." My favorites are the Timeline and the Map.

41. **Tool- Wizer-** https://app.wizer.me/ From the site, "Wizer allows creators of interactive worksheets to add text, video, audio and images. Plus quickly choose from a variety of question types like multiple choice or fill-in-the-blank."

42. **Tool- Flipgrid-** https://info.flipgrid.com/ From the site, "Flipgrid is a simple, free, and accessible video discussion experience for PreK to PhD educators, learners and families. Create a Topic and engage your community...together! Create a discussion Topic. Share it with your learning community. Learners record and share short videos with you and your class."

43. **Tool- Seesaw-** https://web.seesaw.me/ From the site, "Seesaw creates a powerful learning loop between students, teachers, and families. Students use built-in annotation tools to capture what they know in Seesaw's digital portfolio."

44. **Tool- Edpuzzle-** https://edpuzzle.com/about From the site, "Edpuzzle is an easy-to-use platform allowing you to engage every student, one video at a time."

45. **Tool- Play Post It-** www.playposit.com From the site, "**PlayPosit** is an online learning environment to create and share interactive video lessons."

46. **Tool- Kahoot-** https://kahoot.com From the site, "A game based learning platform where users can generate multiple-choice quizzes."

47. **Tool- Canva-** https://www.canva.com From the site, "A graphic design platform that allows you to create everything from social media posts, to posters to vision boards."

48. **Tool- Actively Learn-** https://www.activelylearn.com/ From the site, "Our award-winning digital curriculum drives engagement and equity in class and at home."

49. **Tool- Blackboard-** https://www.blackboard.com/ From the site, "A simpler, more powerful teaching and learning experience that goes beyond the traditional learning management system (LMS)."

50. **Tool- Commonlit-** https://www.commonlit.org/ From the site, "A reading program that reaches all students."

51. **Tool- Turn Off The Lights-** https://www.turnoffthelights.com/ From the site, "Turn Off the Lights Browser extension is a lightweight tool to highlight the video player and darken the rest of the web page."

52. **Tool- Pear Deck-** https://www.peardeck.com/googleslides From the site, "With the Pear Deck for Google Slides Add-on, you can add the magic of formative assessments and interactive questions to your presentations right from Google Slides.

53. **Tool- Simple Audio Recorder-**

https://chrome.google.com/webstore/detail/simple-audio-recorder From the site, "The extension records your voice and saves the recordings as an audio file."

54. **Tool- Newsela-** https://newsela.com/ From the site, "Teachers can search by standard or topic to find content that both supports their curriculum and is engaging and accessible to every learner."

Let's meet Mary Jean – Home Economics Teacher at Leon High School, Tallahassee, Florida.

"Deck the halls with bells of holly, fa la la la la, oh, Hi Y'all! I'm trying to get these holiday decorations up before my class gets here. What year is it? 1960. And believe me, things couldn't get any better in American Education than they are today. Just look at my classroom! I have an oven and six sewing machines. Oh, I love teaching the kids how to bake and sew. It's a chance for them to do something they can take along with them, y'all know, in life. I don't have any problem with the testing they have the students do. It's just that there seems to be a lot of tests now. Since 1916 we have that IQ test to see how good someone remembers and does puzzles, they say. And then, in 1926, they started the SAT, which I had to take to go on to college in Gainesville at the University of Florida. This year, they added science to a test called the ACT, and some universities are looking at that. The best things that have happened for my students have been the funding of school buses in 1919 to transport students to their school buildings and the Smith Hughes Act that funded vocational education in 1917. Many of my students travel out to the vo-tech building on school buses and learn how to do mechanics, woodworking and even how to become beauticians. In 1939 they made yellow the official color of school buses. By the late 1940s, when I was a young girl in school, we had ballpoint pens, and I could get my school lunch at a reduced price thanks to the National School Lunch Act of 1946. Oh, and my older brother was able to attend college on his GI Bill, this bill of rights created in 1944 started helping returning military cover tuition costs. Don't know how he would have gotten anywhere without it. My students keep telling me about the "Information Age" arriving and how electronic computers are going to perform all sorts of tasks for us one day. This chatter all started in 1946 when an Army Major named General Gladeon Barnes turned on a machine in Philadelphia that was created for WWII efforts. Now we have a company named

Texas Instruments making what they call integrated circuits in a second wave of smaller computers. Me, I'm happy with my sewing machines, they sure are faster than hand sewing. And to me that's progress. And I'm happy to have that progress in my classroom."

Discussion Questions

- Do you direct students to online tools that incorporate learning and fun? Always? Sometimes? Rarely?
- How comfortable are you hosting a class session on Zoom?
- Could you teach another teacher how to utilize Google Classroom?

Action Items

- Have your students create a vision board using Canva. Guide them in choosing their goals, selecting inspirational quotes, phrases or words, and finding personal photos or relevant images.
- Invite a co-worker or friend to a Zoom meeting and practice being the host with the most!
- Add interactive questions to your Google Slide presentation with the Pear Deck app. This is one of my favorites.

Fun Fact

In the 1950's themed lunch boxes appeared in school cafeterias, featuring TV shows such as Howdy Doody and Gunsmoke.

PART 5

Are You Feeling Overwhelmed, Stressed And Confused By Virtual Teaching?

The goal of Part 5 is to help you sort out feelings about virtual education and how it impacts your well-being and life.

Virtual teaching can take all the regular stressors of teaching, such as lesson-building and rowdy students, and add even more challenges. All of a sudden, you need to deal with new technology. Each of your students is in a different place, with different distractions. You have little to no way of knowing if a student is looking at his phone or another tab on his browser. Meanwhile, you also have to consider the space you're in. Are you working from home? Is there laundry in the background? Do you have kids at home or animals at home, who might disrupt your call? All of these new challenges can be overwhelming.

If you're a perfectionist, these feelings of stress can be worse. Rather than seeing these new situations as challenges to be overcome, or mistakes that can be forgiven (after all, everyone makes mistakes, so why can't you?), perfectionists tend to feel that they've "failed" more often. Studies show that perfectionistic people - those who feel that they have to be, or at least appear, perfect - have higher rates of anxiety and depression. The **Anxiety and Depression Association of America** reported that 18% of the American population suffers from anxiety. A study of college students found that perfectionism increased significantly over the last three decades. It seems that young people today have higher demands of themselves and others and expect other people to have high demands of them. That's a lot of pressure.

Perfectionism seems to be contagious. Think of it this way. A perfectionist parent might have high expectations of their parenting, but also high expectations of their children. Those high expectations might include expecting their child to receive high grades in school and be engaged in many extracurricular activities. When the child receives a bad mark on a test, the parent might be angry at the child - or at the teacher. In turn, this increases the pressure that the teacher feels to be perfect in his or her work.

To top it all off, perfectionism can be difficult to pinpoint when results aren't clear-cut. If you take a graded test, perfection is clear: you get a score of 100, or at least over 90, right? But we often find that work perfection is harder to define, especially with jobs like teaching. Perfectionists don't let that stop them, though. They will feel extremely disappointed in themselves if students don't like them, or fail their tests, or don't listen in class. Does any of that sound familiar? A perfectionist might have the goal of being loved by all students, but that might not be realistic.

Remember, "perfect is the enemy of good". We often feel that if we didn't do all we set out to do, it's as if we didn't do anything at all. In this process, we ignore everything that we have done or even lose opportunities to take action. Imagine coming home to a sink full of dishes. You know you don't have time to do all of them right now. But perhaps you can wash a few plates and cups and leave the pots for later. If you come in with a perfectionist mindset, you might not touch the sink at all, because you can't complete the job. Yet doing "just a little bit" will lighten the load, make your task easier in the future, and lessen your stress and anxiety about the pile of dishes (because a small pile is less intimidating than a big one).

Teaching-wise, there might be some goals that are imposed upon you, perhaps from the school that you work for. Other goals have to be set by you and require introspection and possibly difficult questions.

What makes you feel that you have succeeded in your teaching? When do you feel that you have failed? How realistic are your goals, and can they be adjusted? Goals that were perhaps realistic during in-person teaching might need to be amended when transitioning to online learning.

One major frustration in transitioning to online teaching is finding out that our previous tried-and-true methods don't work anymore. This is extremely frustrating and overwhelming. In cases like this, we need to find new methods. But perfectionism can keep us stuck if we're afraid to try new things because we're afraid that we'll fail. Yet if we don't try new things, we prevent ourselves from the option of improvement. This negative cycle is hard to break - but luckily, it's not impossible.

Confronting your perfectionistic tendencies can help you change your habits. Learning new tools to use in your online teaching can help you feel more confident. Practicing forgiveness will help you hold your mistakes with more understanding and grace. Making sure you practice self-care and implement a healthy work-life balance will help you regulate your nervous system and become more emotionally regulated.

Implementing everything might seem just as overwhelming as switching over to online teaching, but if you take one thing at a time - and be patient with yourself as you struggle - it will seem a lot more manageable. Many people find it easier to pick one new thing and focus on that. When you feel comfortable with that, you can slowly add new habits.

It can help to remember that as a teacher, you might not know the positive effect that you've had until many years later - and sadly, often not at all. A 12-year-old might not be likely to approach you after class to tell you how much your kind words meant, but that doesn't mean that they won't be remembered. Sometimes our words will encounter resistance in our students, but a seed has still been planted. Just because you can't see something, doesn't mean it isn't there. Focus on being the best that you can be - as long as you give yourself a break and take care of yourself. A teacher-student relationship can be compared to a client-therapist relationship - where the relationship itself is often more important than the tools used. A stressed-out, burnt-out, tired teacher might not be as valuable to her students, even if she stayed up all night creating the coolest presentation. On the other hand, when students see a confident person who takes care of themselves, that teaches them what they can aspire to.

"Everything you want is on the other side of fear."

Jack Canfield

CHAPTER 12

What happens if I fail?

So many times we give up on our ideas and goals before even trying. Teaching online is not a fail or pass situation. It is just another step on the path of change and educational progress that you are completely capable of taking. Keep your worries in check by defining your idea of success in your virtual classroom. Success is not always easy to define. What does online teaching success even look like? Does it look like you in front of your computer, teaching away while your students' faces watch you from their homes in pure excitement and joy, to be learning anything you say? Or does your vision of success look like you in front of your computer, teaching in a completely unfamiliar way, struggling with the technology and the sheer physical distance from your students causing you to feel out of control every time one of the students disappears from their screen, leaving you questioning your entire lesson? Two extremes. Maybe not two good ideas of success, but I have heard teachers say they expect the second version. But, what is your idea of failure at online teaching? No one shows up? They all check out early? They aren't listening to a word you say? Or worse? As **Theo Tsaousides Ph.D., neuropsychologist and author** of *Brainblocks: Overcoming the Seven Hidden Barriers to Success* says, "As long as you continue making an effort, there is no room for failure. When you give up altogether, for no better reason than fear of failing, that's a different story!"

Many teachers are expressing concern about their work-life balance because of the shift to virtual education. Being at home, under one roof with several family members, is not easy if a few guidelines aren't put into place.

In order to maintain work-life balance, keep your private life and school separate. This is a common struggle among teachers and is even more challenging when both work and family life happen at the same place. Being a teacher, it is often part of our job to go the extra mile to benefit our students. Teachers naturally have a tendency to put others' needs before their own. It's not a bad thing. But, especially with virtual teaching, if you don't draw a line between school and home, life could easily get overwhelming. The enormous workload of the job is also a factor, but, you have to accept and understand that you matter too and your wellbeing is your own responsibility. Striking a good balance between school and home is good for both your professional and personal life. Unnecessary stress and burnout are common among teachers that take it too far, but things don't have to be this way.

Do your work only at a designated time and set boundaries. Do you find yourself checking your emails while having dinner? Eat dinner and check emails, but never at the same time. Schedule specific times of your day for work and only do your work during that time, the same goes for relaxation and family time. Having a fixed daily routine can take away your additional stress. Don't hesitate to inform your students that emails will only be answered at specific intervals and only do one thing at a time.

Find time for something you love. Burning both ends of the candle for your profession will only lead to burnout in the long run, even if it feels okay. You need something fun and enjoyable to counter the stress. After your class, put your device aside and go for a bit of exercise, work on an art piece, FaceTime a friend, or enjoy something that makes you feel relaxed.

Learn to say no. Stop taking on work you don't have time for. Again, learn to say "No." This is a key life skill and often the most underappreciated. Do good at your job, but don't expect to be perfect at every aspect of it.

55. **Tip: Atychiphobia- is the fear of failure.** Not wanting to try new things. Not getting involved with challenges. Negative thoughts about oneself. Wild perfectionism- won't do something unless sure they will excel.

56. **Tip: Achievemephobia- is the fear of success.** Continually messing things up, self-sabotage.

CHAPTER 13

How Can You Conquer Fear And Have Fun?

It's no joke that giggling boosts oxygen intake, relaxes muscles and lightens your overall mood. I've spent many years teaching, mentoring and coaching students and adults through ESL, sports and art therapies. I've had the opportunity to work in public and private schools, in fitness clubs, on sports teams, at summer camps and in tutoring centers. I've taught and coached in group settings and with private clients one on one. In all of these settings, I've found that humor solves conflicts, eases anxiety and can stop panic in its tracks.

A good belly laugh increases memory retention. If you can get your students to laugh, they are more likely to remember what you taught them because giggling engages the mind, the physical body and most importantly their hearts. Laughter triggers positive emotions and works as the glue to bond people in relationships. Humorous environments cultivate security and happiness. Humor happens when we expect one scenario or answer and we get a totally different result. Jokes and slapstick comedy work this way. So go ahead, be silly once in a while or everyday.

The new, virtual method of teaching can be challenging for many. A lot of people struggle to convince themselves of their skills and authority when they are put into a new environment. Therefore, it is completely normal that some teachers find virtual teaching a bit more intimidating. However, this fear of changing your ways of working often lasts for a short period and you adjust to it with time and practice. There are several strategies you can use to overcome this fear.

- Start with manageable content. To lessen your fears and make it easier on yourself, start by taking a couple of slides out of your lectures. Teaching in person and online can be a different experience. So, it might be wrong to expect oneself to deliver in the same way as one does in physical classes. To make things easier, try lessening your burden and start with less and manageable course material per lecture.
- Get familiar with the technology. You are still the same teacher with the same knowledge, the only difference now is your medium of communication. Your digital devices and the software you use for teaching are important tools and knowing them thoroughly can make your job easier. Get familiar with platforms you use such as Zoom, Google Classroom, meets, etc., and practice using them.
- Put some extra time into preparation. If you're experiencing difficulties finding a resource during an explanation, students will easily disengage. Not being prepared well for your lectures can be demoralizing for both students and you. Pay special attention to clear instructions and rehearsing your lesson before you start. Being prepared will help you be confident and overcome any fears about your performance as a teacher.

The following are some tips that directly impact your students and reduce stress for you... so go ahead and give them a try.

57. Tip: Be Silly.

Be silly in front of your students. The fear of being laughed at often prevents us from trying new things and doing things at full throttle. Laughing at ourselves is permission to occasionally fall down, to make a mistake, to be clumsy and yes, to fail. But placing such a huge emphasis on the mistake or the failure is what gives it power in the first place. Downplay the value of what you perceive as a failure. Ask yourself, "What is the worst thing that can come of this situation if I fail miserably?"

58. **Tip: Tell Jokes.**

Tell jokes on occasion or on every occasion. Even if you need to buy one of those joke books for kids. If you aren't accustomed to telling your students jokes, this will feel awfully awkward and maybe even staged. It's okay, most of your students will appreciate your effort to lighten the mood, and the rest will wholeheartedly laugh.

59. **Tip: Be Human.**

Your students want to know that you are a human being and that you can relate to them on some level, even if it's only that you are both human. But really, you have so many ways to relate to them. You were a student their age at one time. You share the same concerns about school, friends and family. Topics such as pets, favorite movies, favorite foods, sports, sports teams, and the list goes on and on. Find out what your students are about and relate to them on their level and you become human. If you had to, could you say one personal thing about each of your students that you couldn't know from looking at them?

60. **Idea: Set Positive Goals.**

Set goals phrased in a positive way. Example, "I want my online class to be interesting for my students." Try not to phrase goals with a negative outcome. For example, "I don't want my high school students to be bored with my online class." See the difference? It may seem simple but this re-phrasing is very powerful. It sets the tone for your actions and how you present your material, and guess what? Your students can feel your worry. They will not identify what you are worried about, but they may misinterpret it for your lack of interest in the subject matter, or worse, your lack of interest in their learning.

4 WAYS TO CONQUER FEAR & HAVE FUN
While Teaching Online

1:
BE SILLY

The fear of being laughed at often prevents us from trying new things and doing things at full throttle.

2:
TELL JOKES

Most of your students will appreciate your effort to lighten the mood, and the rest will wholeheartedly laugh..

#3:
BE HUMAN

Find out what your students are about and relate to them on their level and you become human.

4:
SET GOALS

Set goals phrased in a positive way. It sets the tone for your actions and how you present your material..

CHAPTER 14

What about my Well-Being?

If virtual education or the shift from in person teaching to online teaching has caused you stress, take some time to assess your well-being. With every career and occupation there are changes and challenges and online teaching is not an exception. Teachers have told me they come away from their laptops just as drained of energy as they previously did from their physical classrooms.

Virtual teaching can introduce you to new things you were not used to before and being a bit more stressed under such scenarios is completely normal. Complete shifts in routine, challenging methods of teaching, and whatnot. Although it is different from traditional teaching, a lot is still in your hands when it comes to how you deal with it. How you spend and manage your time and what you choose to prioritize, are your responsibility and changing what you can, creates a big difference.

Don't be too hard on yourself if you are not performing as well as you once used to. Things are going to be different and that's alright. So, try to see things under a realistic light, and instead of pushing yourself, be a bit softer. Keep a check on your expectations, and if you're not on top, don't let it get to your head. You will adjust and things will change with time. So, set small, manageable, and realistic goals, that bring joy upon completion.

If you are finding some aspect of your virtual teaching difficult to maintain, instead of stressing over it alone, it's better if you discuss it directly with your colleagues and supervisors. See if any extra duties can be cut and if you can find more resources. See if your routine can be amended to your own liking. And always remember, if you feel like you're having a tough time, reach out to loved ones or a professional counselor that can offer assistance and guidance.

The following tips and ideas are not news, we've all heard them, but it never hurts to stop and ask yourself, "Have I done this for myself lately?" It's also worth mentioning, that the tips and ideas crossover and most likely benefit you in more than one way. For example, spending time doing things that you are good at, such as playing tennis, are good for you emotionally, physically, mentally and socially. Unless you are playing tennis alone, which you probably aren't.

61. Idea: Check Your Emotional Well Being

Do you notice yourself withdrawing from activities you normally enjoy, feeling hopeless or lacking an interest in self-care? These are signs of a less than ideal emotional well-being. It's normal to feel negative occasionally, but when negative thoughts begin to take up most days, you need to gain control of them. Here are a few tips to help you get off the wave of negativity.

- Spend time doing activities you're already good at. It's a confidence booster.
- Talk about how you feel with someone other than a family member.
- Keep a journal of your daily outlook on your job, family, finances and life.
- Know when and where to seek professional help if needed.

62. Idea: Check Your Physical Well Being

Do you feel sluggish, distracted or restless while teaching? These are signs of a less than ideal physical well-being. It's normal to be tired some days, we all are. But if your tiredness occurs every day and for long periods of time, you need to make some changes. After all, your physical well being is not only, the absence of disease. Physical well-being is a balance of physical activity and nutrition. It affects your mental and emotional well-being as well. Here are a few tips to help you feel alert, focused and calm.

- Add or begin an exercise program that involves cardio, strength training and flexibility.
- Check your calorie intake and plan meals ahead of time.
- When not teaching or planning lessons, stay off social media and technology altogether.
- Find a partner to hold you accountable.

63. Idea: Check Your Mental Well Being

Feeling blue and not like you? Experiencing daily bouts of frustration, boredom, anxiety or panic? These are signs that your mental well-being is at risk. It's normal to feel blue when something terrible happens, but when you can't identify reasons for feeling this way, you need to check in with yourself. Here are a few tips to keep you mentally ready to take on any challenge.

- Continue to learn.
- Most educators continue to learn throughout their lives. If you haven't learned anything new and outside of your expertise, look into a completely fresh subject like a new language, how to draw figures or about the history of a culture you are not familiar with.
- Creative expression and mental well-being are linked.
- Write a poem, draw someone, and paint a landscape.
- The flavonoids and caffeine in dark chocolate boost alertness.
- Eat two squares of dark chocolate in the afternoon for, "a pick me up."
- List 3 things you are grateful each day in a gratitude notebook. When you are feeling extra blue, read the list.
- Enjoy reading books that are NOT career oriented.
- Go to your local library and ask to check out the fiction book of the month. Most libraries feature an employee favorite or classic.

64. Idea: Check Your Social Well Being

When was the last time you got together with friends? Is your family nearby or does it require travel to visit them? It's normal to lose track of time and need to catch up with family and friends. But, getting together with them is not only about your relationships with them, it's about you building social time for yourself. Here are a few tips to keep you socially engaged and active.

- Social well-being is a good indicator of mental well-being.
- Characteristics of being socially well adjusted are: agreeable, open, responsible and hardworking.
- Look at your calendar and schedule social activities. Even an evening walk and talk through the neighborhood counts.
- Make every effort to stay in touch with family and friends. This can include snail mail, email, text, phone, Zoom, and in person socializing.

Let's meet Kate- Teacher at the Virginia School for the Deaf and Blind, Staunton, Virginia.

"Hello there, come on in, welcome to our classroom. We're creating Valentines on the computers, we can't forget about Valentine's Day! What year is it? Oh, 1989. And believe me, things couldn't be any better in American education than they are today. My students really enjoy using the school's computers. They installed Microsoft Windows 1.0 and it's amazing what we can do now. They call them personal computers, but we share them in this room we call a computer lab, you know, like a biology lab or physics lab. Except, we only work on the computers in this room. In 1972, Texas Instruments started selling hand held calculators, I mean it fits in my lunch tote. But it gets better... in 1977 that Apple company created the first personal computer and then the very next year, IBM came out with their version. I've personally never seen an Apple computer. Progress really happened in 1963, when we began to refer to students with brain based disabilities as having a learning disability. And then, in 1965, the Department of Health and Human Services created Head

Start, a program to prepare low-income children for elementary school. In 1971, a law was passed to provide free education for the mentally disabled. It seems we've become more empathetic and inclusive, but there is always room for growth. Speaking of growth, I was able to attend Columbia College for my degree, they were the last Ivy League school to go co-ed in 1983. Oh! Yes, before I forget, this building I'm in has a metal detector. Just installed a few months ago. Also, I heard about this thing called an e-book from one of my professors at the University of Phoenix, where I'm earning my master's degree. And get this, I take my courses on the world wide web, yep, right on my new Gateway computer! For me, progress is amazing!"

Discussion Questions

- Do you begin and end your teaching day stressed, exhausted or emotional? Always? Sometimes? Rarely?
- How often do you share a laugh with your students?
- Has physical activity been a part of your daily schedule on school days?

Action Items

- Have your students take responsibility for part of their learning. Empower them by assigning small tasks that you would normally perform for a lesson. For example students could: prepare the PowerPoint presentation, come up with questions about the topic, decide which websites, apps and resources should be used for the lesson, utilize self-assessments to contribute to the teacher assessment, divide the information up and teach each other mini-lessons.
- Ask another teacher to listen to you bounce ideas around and hash out concerns you have about online teaching. Having someone in your situation listen goes a long way in releasing anxiety and tension.
- Write down at least three positively phrased goals for your online teaching experience.

Fun Fact

Since the 1880's, children have been asked, "What is your favorite subject in school?" The answer, by an overwhelming majority, is recess.

References

Tsaousides, Theo, *Brainblocks: Overcoming the Seven Hidden Barriers to Success* (Prentice Hall Press, 2015).

Anxiety and Depression Association of America: Facts & Statistics. Retrieved August 2020 at https://adaa.org/about-adaa/press-room/facts-statistics

PART 6

How Can I Accommodate All Of My Learners?

The goal of Part 6 is to provide you with a list of websites and apps that can be incorporated into most subject areas and assist learners with special needs.

Learning online can be daunting, but even more so for students with special needs who need structure, personal guidance, reassurances and clear instructions. During the global pandemic, teachers and educators have witnessed all students struggle physically, mentally, emotionally and socially. However, those who have struggled the most are students with special needs. The following areas can be used to support your students with special needs, helping them to achieve their learning goals.

Structure to the day – For a student with Autism or ADHD, a daily pattern has been established when they attend school each day. The students meet friends and peers, go to the same classrooms, eat their lunch in the same place, and recognize where to get help and support if needed. Learning online, strips away that support network, because face to face contact has been minimized. As a result, routine has been upset and needs to be re-established within the home environment, creating a sense of control for the student. Once the routine has been settled, online learning can begin to show its advantages. It is important to encourage students to do things they love, and what they are interested in, therefore not forcing the learning, so a new pattern can be fully developed, and a learning environment can be established.

Being organized – A common trait with special needs is disorganization, not only in the ways of thinking but also with physical items. It is important to ensure that students with special needs have a clear idea about what they are to learn, how long to spend on each section, learning outcomes that they need to achieve, along with the necessary equipment such as books, paper, stationary and access to essential websites to help ease access issues. Taking time to get organized will help plan future work, the ability to meet deadlines and help with time management.

Technology – The vast range of technology that is available for students with special needs is outstanding. Making sure that your students know there is support for them is something that every teacher should focus on. Services such as assistive technology like text to speech, speech to text, online dictionaries, audio captions, screen readers to decipher text-based phrases and spell check are some vital tools for students with Dyslexia. Speech to text, voice recorded notes, and typing tools are vital for students with Dysgraphia. Students with hearing issues should have access to transcriptions, closed captions for lectures, and support on video calls. Students with visual impairments can have access to Braille keyboards, text-to-speech facilities, modified teaching resources and printing access to improve their learning. With the technology available, all students with special needs can succeed with the resources that are available to them.

IEPs – Each student with special needs should have an Individual Educational Plan. This paperwork focuses on the child's needs, strategies to help them learn, what areas of weakness need be addressed, what methods of teaching are successful and targets for future learning, along with an evaluation for future progress. IEPs should be made available to each teacher and then be adapted and differentiated so that the best methods and resources are utilized for all learning needs and abilities.

Flexibility – One of the major benefits with online learning is that it can be made as flexible as the student needs. If the student with special needs is struggling and can not keep up with the pace, or needs to revisit a topic to allow for a deeper understanding, with online learning it is possible. Tasks can also be repeated as many times as required until knowledge and understanding is gained. Being able to stop and have a break is also a great tool to allow students to have a rest, refocus and return to their learning, avoiding burnout and lack of motivation. With the ease of restarting the lessons at a time that suits the student, they can feel positive and enjoy their time learning. Online learning is convenient for students with special needs, allowing them to work at their own pace, and at a time that suits them.

Online learning for students with special needs must be completed in a planned and organized way to ensure that all learners excel. The advancement of technology allows for students to be in control of their learning, avoiding any hurdles in their way, while supporting and enabling them to learn. Teachers will need to take students' learning habits into consideration to ensure that all students can reach their target grades while enjoying learning online.

This list is not exhaustive of all of the great websites and apps available, but merely a glimpse into the never ending resources the internet has to offer. Some websites and apps are better than others and may work for some teachers and not for others. One particular concern I hear repeatedly from parents of children being schooled online, is that they are left in the dark when it comes to the technology their sometimes young children are expected to navigate. As **Melanie Kitchen stated in an article written by Jennifer Gonzalez in Cult of Pedagogy,** "Provide parent tech training. Parents will be better able to support students if they understand how to use the technology, so provide them with tutorials on the tech you use, including whatever platform you use to disseminate information."

EFFECTIVE USE OF TECHNOLOGY

Technology is the device used to accomplish a learning outcome, not the end result.

A Blog

Should:
- Start new discussions.
- Be Collaborative with others.
- Ask new questions
- Find new answers.

Do you want them to start a blog for the sake of blogging? Nope!

Digital Portfolio

Should:
- Be ever changing and growing.
- Encourage interaction with others.
- Open their minds to the possibilities of what they can share with the world.

Is this task solely to display their work? Nope!

At the very core of this topic, accommodating all learners, is the basic belief that all learners deserve to be provided with what they need. So, how can you accommodate all learners? Begin by asking yourself, "What do I want my students to do with the technology they utilize? Do you want them to start a blog for blogging's sake? Or do you hope that by creating a blog they start new discussions, collaborate with others, ask new questions and find new answers? When students build a digital portfolio of their work on any of the many platforms available to do such a task, is the task solely to display their work? Hopefully the portfolio they build is ever changing and growing. And maybe the work they choose to upload encourages interaction with others. Perhaps, their portfolio opens their minds to the possibilities of what they can share with the world. So you see, technology is the device used to accomplish a learning outcome, not the end result. From what most educators tell me, whatever technology students have access to, they will embrace. My first hand experience with two teenagers at home is that technology is paramount. There is no doubt that the future of my children's chosen career paths will involve technology. Teachers can connect and accommodate their students by utilizing all the technology they can maneuver.

"When educating the minds of our youth, we must not forget to educate their hearts."

Dalai Lama

CHAPTER 15

What Are Some Great
Websites By Subject?

The following lists, in both chapters fifteen and sixteen, are not exhaustive of all of the wonderful websites for educators and their students, but rather a selection of sites recommended frequently and with enthusiasm. Also, as the sites are updated and changed often, this list is current only at the time of publication.

Math Websites

65. **Tool - Freckle** - https://www.freckle.com/math/ From the site, "Freckle's Math tools give educators everything they need to reach each student at their own level in Math from grades K-9."

66. **Tool - Math Drills** - https://www.math-drills.com/ From the site, "Math-Drills.com includes over 57 thousand free math worksheets that may be used to help students learn math."

67. **Tool - Aplus Math** - https://www.varsitytutors.com/aplusmath From the site, "Interactive math resources for teachers, parents, and students featuring free math worksheets, math games, math flashcards, and more."

Language Websites

68. **Tool - Read, Write Think** - http://www.readwritethink.org/ From the site, "Lessons, interactives, calendar activities, and more, right at your fingertips."

69. **Tool – Funbrain** - https://www.funbrain.com/ From the site, "Funbrain, created for kids in grades Pre-K through 8, offers hundreds of free interactive games, books, videos, and printables that help kids develop skills in math, reading, problem-solving, and literacy."

70. **Tool – Brainpop** - https://www.brainpop.com/ From the site, "A trusted learning resource supporting core and supplemental subjects, reaching millions of learners worldwide."

Art Websites

71. **Tool - Google Arts and Culture** - https://artsandculture.google.com/ From the site, "Google Arts & Culture features content from over 2000 leading museums and archives."

72. **Tool - National Gallery of Art** - https://www.nga.gov/ From the site, "The nation's museum–preserves, collects, exhibits, and fosters an understanding of works of art."

73. **Tool - 3Dux/Design** - https://www.3duxdesign.com/ From the site, "The 3DuxDesign award-winning Architectural Modeling System offers an engaging, hands-on tool that blends art, design and creative play with STEM learning."

Chemistry Websites

74. **Tool - Physics Central** - https://www.physicscentral.com/ From the site, "Physics Central runs programs for all ages with the goal of making physics fun and interesting for everyone."

75. **Tool - Institute of Physics** - https://www.iop.org/education From the site, "We work to promote, develop and support excellent physics teaching through networks, CPD events and proven resources."

76. **Tool - PHET Interactive Simulations -**
https://phet.colorado.edu/ From the site, "Interactive simulations
for science and math."

Music Websites

77. **Tool- Beatlab -** https://www.beatlab.com/ From the site,
"Beatlab is the easiest way to create music and share it with your
friends."

78. **Tool- Smart Music -** https://www.smartmusic.com/ From the
site, "SmartMusic is music learning software for educators and
students. Make practicing and tracking student progress easy and
fun."

79. **Tool- AudioSauna -** http://www.audiosauna.com/ From the
site, "AudioSauna is a free music software for making songs online."

Social Studies Websites

80. **Tool - CNN Student News-** https://www.cnn.com/cnn10 From
the site, "CNN Student News is a ten-minute, commercial-free, daily
news program designed for middle and high school classes."

81. **Tool- iCivics -** https://www.icivics.org/ From the site, "Free
lesson plans and games for learning civics."

82. **Tool- PBS Learning Social Studies-**

https://www.pbslearningmedia.org/subjects/social-studies/ From
the site, "Discover thousands of social studies activities, lessons, and
interactive resources for all grades, all aligned to state and national
standards."

History Websites

83. **Tool - Historic Newspapers -** https://www.historic-
newspapers.com/ From the site, "Any date, any title: revel in the past
with newspapers from the world's largest physical archive of over
200000 original newspapers."

84. **Tool - The History Engine -** https://historyengine.richmond.edu/ From the site, "The History Engine is a collection of thousands of historical "episodes" that paints a wide-ranging portrait of the past that is freely available to scholars, teachers, and the general public."

85. **Tool - Zoom In -** http://zoomin.edc.org/ From the site, "Classroom Ready Lessons. Immerse students in highly interactive, document-based inquiry lessons designed by historians and teachers."

Science Websites

86. **Tool - Mystery Science-** https://mysteryscience.com/ From the site, "Mystery Science offers open-and-go lessons that inspire kids to love science. The hook, visuals, and activity have all been prepared for you."

87. **Tool - Science Buddies -** https://www.sciencebuddies.org/ From the site, "Free Topic Selection Wizard, science fair project ideas, step by step how to do a science fair project, Ask an Expert discussion board, and science fair tips."

88. **Tool - Mosa Mack -** https://mosamack.com/ From the site, "Animated mysteries + collaborative labs + engineering challenges for your science classroom. Try our inquiry-based NGSS units for students in 4th-8th grade."

Physical Education Websites

89. **Tool - Shape America -** https://www.shapeamerica.org/ From the site, "The leading website for health education and PE teachers."

90. **Tool - We Are teachers -** https://www.weareteachers.com/ From the site, "Ideas, Inspiration, and Giveaways for Teachers."

91. **Tool - Gopher Sport -** https://www.gophersport.com/ From the site, "The leader in quality Physical Education, Athletics, and Fitness equipment."

CHAPTER 16

What Are The Best Apps For Learners with Special Needs?

Apps That Help Learners with Writing

92. Tool - ABC Pocket Phonics -
https://apps.apple.com/us/app/pocketphonics-basic-edition/id299342927 From the site, "This phonics based application combines letter sounds, letter writing, and 170 first words to help teach reading."

93. Tool - Alpha Writer - https://www.educationalappstore.com/ From the site, "A Montessori-style learning app that helps kids learn letter sounds and teaches them how to form words."

94. Tool - iWrite Words -
https://apps.apple.com/us/app/iwritewords-handwriting-game/id307025309. From the site, "A handwriting app where users trace words, letters, and numbers at their own pace in order to become more familiar with the alphabet and numeral system."

95. Tool - The Writing Machine -
https://apps.apple.com/us/app/the-writing-machine/id438108325 From the site, "The Writing Machine is designed to start introducing your child to these pre-literacy concepts of print, text, reading and writing."

96. **Tool- Letter School-** https://www.letterschool.org/ From the site, "How to write letters and numbers."

Apps That Help Autistic Learners

96. **Tool - Speech With Milo -** http://www.speechwithmilo.com/ From the site, "Created by a licensed Speech-Language Pathologist as a versatile and entertaining speech therapy tool for children."

97. **Tool - Words On Wheels -** https://www.wordsonwheels.org/ From the site, "Words on Wheels is an augmentative and alternative communication (AAC) app for the iPad that helps children with speech problems."

98. **Tool - See.Touch.Learn -**

https://learningworksforkids.com/apps/see-touch-learn/ From the site, "A great educational tool for Alternative Learners. This app replaces and enhances the traditional picture card teaching method."

99. **Tool - Verbal Me -** https://apps.apple.com/us/app/verbal-me/id495853688 From the site, "An app designed by special needs teachers for their students."

100. **Tool - Autism iHelp -**

https://apps.apple.com/us/app/autism-ihelp-play/id521485216 From the site, "Autism iHelp is a vocabulary teaching aid developed by parents of a child with Autism and a speech-language pathologist."

Apps That Help Students with Dyslexia

101. **Tool - Dyslexia Quest -** https://apps.apple.com/us/app/dyslexia-quest/id448166369 From the site, "A game designed to help assess your child's memory and listening skills."

102. **Tool – Dyseggxia -** https://search.bridgingapps.org/apps/d30b68b5-afb8-7b98-ce57-

aef00cf05afc From the site, "A mobile game that helps children with dyslexia overcome their reading and writing problems."

103. Tool - Read 2 Me -

https://chrome.google.com/webstore/detail/read-to-me/nalcmippmnicanikekphpdmmcgoojjlm?hl=en From the site, "A text to speech Chrome extension for reading out loud any text in your browser in many languages."

104. Tool - Happy Math Multiplication Rhymes -

https://apps.apple.com/us/app/happymath-multiplication-rhymes-free/id511973121 From the site, "Based on a proven educational principle ~ memorization by association."

105. Tool - DD"s Dictionary: A Dyslexic Dictionary -

https://apps.apple.com/us/app/dds-dictionary-a-dyslexics-dictionary/id590239077 From the site, "Allows independent discovery of an unknown spelling or a quick check of an uncertain word."

Apps That Help The Visually Impaired

106. Tool - Light Detector - https://apps.apple.com/us/app/light-detector/id420929143 From the site, "Transforms any natural or artificial light source it encounters into sound."

107. Tool - Be My Eyes- Helping Blind See -

https://www.bemyeyes.com/ From the site, "Whether you need a pair of sharp eyes or have some sight to lend, Be My Eyes is a simple, free tool to help people see the world better, together."

108. Tool - Color ID -

https://play.google.com/store/apps/details?id=com.hempton.colorid&hl=en_US From the site, "Colorblind? Need to settle a color dispute with your friends? Look no further! Point your phone at anything and get its exact color."

109. **Tool - A Talking Calculator** (many brand names) - https://www.amazon.com/ From the site, "A talking calculator has a built-in speech synthesizer that reads aloud each number, symbol, or operation key a user presses; it also vocalizes the answer to the problem."

110. **Tool- Dragon Dictation** - https://shop.nuance.com/ From the site, "Dictate documents, send email, search the Web, and more - at home or in school."

Let's meet Amanda - Teacher at Monta Loma Elementary School, Mountain View, California.

"Today is one of those bittersweet days where I feel sad to leave but excited to go. It's the last day of the school year. What year is it? 2003. Okay, let me explain. I just finished my first year as a teacher, and it was wonderful. I'm packing up my personal belongings now because I committed to a two year teaching position with Teach for America, and they are sending me off to Arizona! Teach for America is a non-profit working towards educational equality and well, I just feel like this is a great humanitarian opportunity. But, wow, am I going to miss this elementary and my second graders. Plus, I don't think I'll have access to all of the wonderful technology I have here. Take for example my white board, this cool replacement for the messy chalk boards came out in 1994. And get this, in the library they have a Smart Board, a crazy interactive whiteboard that you can just touch to operate. Our community also offers a public charter school, this is an option that offers tuition free education as an alternative to the district you live in. The first charter school opened in Minnesota in 1992 when I was just a kid myself. It took a few years until we had one here in Silicon Valley. The first version of the Netscape web browser was released in 1994 and since then we've upgraded to Netscape 6. It looks like AOL will close Netscape soon because of competitors. In 1998 we started using Google for everything. Google was started near my home in a garage in Menlo Park. The students love to google topics and I use google for recipes at home. A major shift has been online education. The first completely online high school was Compu High in 1994, and since then there have been more popping up online. In 1995 Georgia became the first state to fund a preschool program. Now the school districts must make "adequate yearly progress" to conform to the NCLB, No Child Left Behind Act, and this means our students are tested for achievement and teachers are held accountable. But what I'm excited about is the online learning I mentioned. This year, they formed the corporate entity, the International Association for K-12 Online Learning. And thanks to that progress they will continue to explore and enhance online teaching methods and opportunities. This makes me wonder if one day I will teach my young students from a computer screen. Yes, it really makes me wonder.

Discussion Questions

- Do you have an arsenal of learning activities for learners with special needs?
- Have you made cross-curricular teaching part of your curriculum?
- Are websites and apps a substitute for human interaction & education ?

Action Items

- Have your students evaluate the websites and apps you introduce. Ask for their opinion on the app's function, design, how navigable it is and about its fun factor.
- Offer parents a demonstration via Loom or a downloadable PDF of the apps, tools and technology you plan to utilize in class. A brief five minute mini-lesson will help parents feel connected and better equipped while their child is online learning with you.
- Utilize websites and apps only when needed. Set time allotments and keep tabs on how often you rely on them in lessons.

Fun Fact

Anti-school song lyrics have been around for decades in songs such as "She's Sexy & 17" by the Stray Cats in 1983 and "School's Out" by Alice Cooper in 1972. One of the first recorded musicians to popularize the subject was Chuck Berry with his 1957 song "School Days."

References

Gonzalez, Jennifer. (July 5, 2020) "9 Ways Online Teaching Should Be Different from Face-To-Face." Interview with Melanie Kitchen, retrieved on Cult of Pedagogy, August 2020 at:

https://www.cultofpedagogy.com/9-ways-online-teaching/

CONCLUSION

Let's wrap this up. In conclusion, I'd like to review the goals of this book. In doing so, you can assess how far you've come mentally, emotionally, and physically with virtual education from prior to reading this book and moving forward. But before doing so, I want to touch upon the reason why this book exists in the first place: change. We've all heard of the old saying, "The only thing constant in life is change". I have always felt that change is encoded into the very fabric of the universe itself. Every second of every day, time moves forward, and with it, change happens. Things are always transforming into other things, be it on the molecular level or in our society. We have all experienced it in the past and we keep experiencing it on a regular basis in the present. Change is inevitable and the only thing we can really do is adapt to it.

From my experiences and observations, I have come to know and understand that teachers, as a group of people, have always been resilient and adaptable. And if you think about it, it only makes sense. Teachers are tasked with imparting knowledge in society. And as with every other thing, our pool of knowledge constantly gets updated and revised. This is literally how the human race keeps moving forward. We keep discovering or inventing new things and so, our collective knowledge just keeps on increasing. It is us teachers that are tasked with spreading this ever-evolving pool of knowledge. On top of this, the methods of teaching have also always been evolving. So, you could say that being resilient, vigilant, or keeping with the times, comes with the profession itself. Because of all the teachers that I have worked with and had the pleasure of knowing or meeting, I have a firm belief that teachers are some of the first people in society who respond to change.

In 2020, the COVID-19 pandemic brought more changes than have ever happened in such a short period of time. As a race, we almost came to a halt. It was our resilience that kept us going, adapting to the situation, and finding new ways of doing things. Teachers have been able to do the same. Social distancing norms and the closure of schools and colleges meant finding new ways to continue teaching and learning. The switch to virtual education was the only natural and most logical next step. The technology to facilitate this has been around for a long time and it was merely waiting for us to adopt it.

I understand that many changes can be a bit unsettling at first, but it is in times like these that we need to keep going on anyway. If you believe in yourself, you can overcome any challenge that comes in your way. Don't we all teach this to our students? I know the situation is quite tricky but it is also amusing in a way. Teachers are always motivating and inspiring their students to be better versions of themselves, to grow and learn new things and adapt them into their lives for better results. To create value for the world, so that everyone can be better for it. And now, it is teachers themselves that might need some motivation to do the same! This is what I hope to accomplish with this book. I thought I could motivate or inspire you to believe in your abilities, to rise to the occasion and focus on ways you can transition to the new way of educating students.

You see, we have all had experiences where we thought a particular situation or challenge was just insurmountable, but later on, we managed to defeat it anyway and came out stronger due to that experience. In our minds, we might sometimes overestimate the difficulty of the challenge we face and underestimate our own abilities. You might especially be prone to doing this in times like these, where there is a generally gloomy mood all around the world. But as I said, teachers as a group of people are highly adaptable and somehow they always find a way. You have immense experience as adults and figuring out how to help your students is well within your capability. Your students count on you and this knowledge alone should be enough for anyone to feel motivated to do whatever they must to keep teaching. After all, it's about the future of so many young people. People who will shape our world in new ways. People who hold the promise of solving the biggest problems that humanity faces. It could all start with you believing in your ability and finding ways to deal with this change that has been put upon you, so that you can continue to do what you do and embrace the progress with open arms in the process.

It is often said that necessity is the mother of invention. Right now, the necessity of education is to adapt to the virtual model. Who knows when things will be back to the way they were. It only makes logical sense to embrace progress and use the tools that are available to us today to keep the light of education on. In a way, this is very exciting. We might be in the midst of a revolution that could define the way education systems work for decades to come. There is an interesting saying, "nothing can stop an idea whose time has come". Maybe, the time of virtual education is finally upon us and we should welcome it wholeheartedly. Who knows, it might open new doors to better ways of imparting knowledge. It might reveal things that we never thought were possible. It could also make education more accessible and affordable for countless students out there for whom finances act as a barrier. Yes, it might take some time, but it will all be worth it.

My hopes are that you've opened your mind to the immense possibilities that come with online teaching and have been able to figure out ways to incorporate some of your most beloved in-person teaching practices along the way. It's totally okay if you're not able to figure out every single detail in a single go. Changes like these take time to take final form and patience is key during the whole process. For instance, I have been told and have experienced firsthand that the single most difficult component of virtual education is self-regulation. Keeping ourselves and our students from being distracted by other devices, pets, family members, chores, doorbells, and beautiful sunny days, is difficult for adults and even more challenging for kids and teens. But in time, we will all learn to deal with challenges like this.

There is also a psychological side to this that often goes unnoticed. For many people, the transition period of driving to the school where they teach, arriving in the parking lot, walking up the sidewalk, and entering the building signifies a shift to work and school. It allows the brain to transition from personal life to work/school life. This time to shift gears is taken away when teaching from home.

Staying at home makes it difficult to put on and wear your teacher hat. To overcome this, you could create a routine that resembles that of leaving for school. Maybe take a short walk before entering your remote teaching space. And for goodness sake, get dressed in something other than pajamas or sweats. When I recently met with educators who are new to teaching online, a few of them admitted to wearing the same clothes to sleep and teach! This defeats the whole point of what you are trying to accomplish... being a great online teacher. If you aren't taking a few minutes to "get ready", you can't possibly feel presentable, professional, and motivated. So, now that you've all realized you need to brush your teeth and put some pants on to succeed at online teaching, let's review what each part of this book covered and double-check that you've accomplished at least a few of the action items.

"The secret of change is to focus all of your energy, not on fighting the old, but on building the new." **Socrates**

CHAPTER 17

Let's Reflect

Let's reflect. The two most important takeaways of teaching remotely are clear communication and consistent routines. The following four ideas have been staples in brick and mortar settings but need to be carried over into the virtual classroom whenever possible.

1. Have students set personal educational goals,
2. Allow for self-directed education,
3. Connect the curriculum to the students' lives, making it relevant to them.
4. Involve students in their own critique and assessment.

Below you will find the opening sentence of each of the six parts of this book. Read each goal and decide if you've made any progress in your heart, your mind, or with your curriculum and lesson planning.

The goal of **Part 1** is that you become more familiar with the changes in American education and how the changes became milestones of progress. My ultimate hope is that you remain open to the changes coming your way and enjoy some of the changes with an open heart. Do you feel that you've attained any headway in this area? Have you implemented any of the tips, tools or ideas? What was your reaction to this part of the book? What additional actions have you taken?

The goal of **Part 2** is to demonstrate that your students want to be engaged, are open to being engaged in online education, and it is possible to engage students in every online lesson you teach. Do you feel that you've attained any headway in this area? Have you implemented any of the tips, tools or ideas? What was your reaction to this part of the book? What additional actions have you taken?

The goal of **Part 3** is to demonstrate that your online students are open to connecting with you virtually and that there are ways to connect that will create similar experiences and bonds to those in a brick and mortar classroom. Do you feel that you've attained any headway in this area? Have you implemented any of the tips, tools or ideas? What was your reaction to this part of the book? What additional actions have you taken?

The goal of **Part 4** is to present tools that will open new ways to enhance your online teaching, be creative with how you present your curriculum and feel that you are giving your student the best virtual education you can. Do you feel that you've attained any headway in this area? Have you implemented any of the tips, tools or ideas? What was your reaction to this part of the book? What additional actions have you taken?

The goal of **Part 5** is to help you sort out feelings about virtual education and how it impacts your well-being and life. Do you feel that you've attained any headway in this area? Have you implemented any of the tips, tools or ideas? What was your reaction to this part of the book? What additional actions have you taken?

The goal of **Part 6** is to provide you with a list of websites and apps that can be incorporated into most subject areas and assist learners with special needs AND guide you on how to incorporate the technology into your classroom and school community including parents. Do you feel that you've attained any headway in this area? Have you implemented any of the tips, tools or ideas? What was your reaction to this part of the book? What additional actions have you taken?

Discussion Questions

- Do you believe that you can manage the changes required of you as an educator?

- How has progress during your teaching career helped your teaching goals?
- What tips and ideas do you want to embrace and put into action?

Action Items

- List ten things that have progressed during your teaching career.
- Ask for help. Ask for help with the technology, translating your curriculum, managing an online schedule, and balancing your new career with your life.
- If you have a difficult time finding help, consider the companion course and coaching available to readers of this book.

Fun Fact

A recent poll asked participants to list reasons why they remember their favorite teacher. Funny and caring were the top two reasons named by the majority.

THANK YOU FOR READING MY BOOK!

FREE BONUS GIFT

As a thank you gift for purchasing this book, there are a few free gifts, exclusive to readers of *Dynamite Online Teacher- 110 Tips, Tools & Ideas To Connect With Your Students Online & Embrace Progress.*

To Download Now, Visit:

http://www.DynamiteOnlineTeacher.com/dh-freegift

I appreciate your interest in my book and I value your feedback as it helps me improve future versions of this book. I would appreciate it if you could leave your invaluable review on Amazon.com with your feedback. Thank you!

www.ingramcontent.com/pod-product-compliance
Lightning Source LLC
LaVergne TN
LVHW041212050326
832903LV00021B/594